Move

Pivotal Solutions For Your Life

Windy Elstermeier

Pivotal Solutions

Copyright © 2023 by Windy Elstermeier

All rights reserved.

No portion of this book may be reproduced in any form without written permission from the publisher or author, except as permitted by U.S. copyright law.

This publication is designed to provide accurate and authoritative information in regard to the subject matter covered. It is sold with the understanding that neither the author nor the publisher is engaged in rendering legal, investment, accounting or other professional services. While the publisher and author have used their best efforts in preparing this book, they make no representations or warranties with respect to the accuracy or completeness of the contents of this book and specifically disclaim any implied warranties of merchantability or fitness for a particular purpose. No warranty may be created or extended by sales representatives or written sales materials. The advice and strategies contained herein may not be suitable for your situation. You should consult with a professional when appropriate. Neither the publisher nor the author shall be liable for any loss of profit or any other commercial damages, including but not limited to special, incidental, consequential, personal, or other damages.

Book Cover by Rachel Korpella, Owner of Korpella Design
https://korpelladesign.com

1.2.23VOL1 edition 2023

Contents

Dedication	V
Introduction	VI
1. Get Out of Your Own Way	1
Notes Page	15
2. Let it Go!	16
Notes Page	27
3. The Big F's	28
Notes Page	44
4. Step by Step Walking Out of Overwhelm	45
Notes Page	62
5. Attitude Is Everything	63
Notes Page	79

6. Lifting the Weight	80
Notes Page	96
7. You Are Unique	97
Notes Page	109
8. The Green Monster	110
Notes Page	125
9. Ask for What You Want	126
Notes Page	142
10. Financial Security Matters	143
Notes Page	155
11. Dig Out the GRIT!	156
Notes Page	166
12. Build a Support System	167
Notes Page	185
13. Who Do You Want to Be?	186
Notes Page	199

To my readers,

Thank you!

Introduction

After reading this book you will be inspired and motivated to be powerful in your own space. I will give you pivotal solutions in 3 to 5 steps to break down the barriers in your way. You will be able to use them to take your life to the next level. You will look back in a year and be proud of the progress you have made.

I am writing this book for you because you matter.

You could be:

- A victim of your own negative self-talk

- Stuck in a world of hurt and anger

- Afraid of failure

- Feel like everything is impossible

You might:

- Need an attitude adjustment
- Need support
- Spend too much time focused on what others have or what is not fair in life
- Need to build financial security

You might have trouble:

- Believing in yourself
- Seeing the value you bring
- Asking for what you want
- Finding the grit inside yourself

We all have things holding us back. Once you read this book about my successes and failures and how they might apply to your life, you will be able to use these pivotal solutions I have provided to get out of your own way and build the confidence to start moving toward achieving your dreams.

I hope that someday I meet you and you can share your story with me and the things you have changed that gave you the power to move forward.

This book will serve you best if you read one chapter at a time and then give yourself some time to go and practice it in the real world.

This book is not a one-time read. It is a tool designed to help you as often as you need.

I recommend this book to be used in a way that truly makes a difference for you.

That could be by reading it once and then going back and finding the chapter or chapters that are meaningful to you and practicing them in your day-to-day life. Or by reading one chapter at a time and giving yourself some time to go and practice it in the real world.

You will need to:

- Pay attention to what you are doing and

when.

- Learn and practice how to manage it.

- Think about it.

- Roll it around.

- Take what you learn in this book and gain real-world experience in it.

- Deep dive into a specific area and read more books about that topic.

This book will give you a window to see that we are all flawed human beings and we all need help and support. Give yourself grace.

Chapter One

Get Out of Your Own Way

Behold Self-talk

I worked for a Fortune 500 company, and we were on a corporate jet flying to Georgia to open the 200th location of our new small format. I was listening to an article about self-talk. It said to write down all the terrible things you were saying to yourself in your head. Put it on paper.

I thought, "Okay, I can do that."

2 MOVE

I did not think it was a big deal. I was a highly successful career woman, after all, I was on a corporate jet, and I am a pretty positive person.

I got out my cell phone, opened my notes app, and started writing the things I was worried about in my head.

Take a minute and find something to write on. If you have a hard copy of this book you have a note page after each chapter to start with. Now give yourself a few minutes to ponder and make a list of all the stuff. My list went something like this.

- My pants don't match.
- My necklace is too long.
- My breath stinks.
- My butt is too fat for the seat.
- I might have to pee.
- These people just brought me out of pity.
- I don't really deserve to be here.
- My hair is not clean enough.

- My fat rolls might be showing.

- I wonder what my boss is thinking.

- No one is talking. Should I be talking?

I found the list not only shocking but incredibly embarrassing. The list went on and on. I could not believe all the negative stuff floating in my head. How in the world did I ever get anything done with all that going on? As I was writing the stuff in my head down, I quickly started debunking it.

To debunk means "to expose falseness or hollowness of a myth, idea, or belief." ("Debunker - Wikipedia")

One side of the page was the crap in my head and the other side was the reality or a solution. I could not believe all the mean things I was saying to myself. I was a bully who was saying horrible things to myself. If you have not done this exercise. Do it! I mean it. Write it down! Then maybe burn it. Because it will be a horrible list you would never want anyone else to read.

4   MOVE

Here is what debunking looks like.

- My pants don't match – I was wearing a white shirt. Everything matches white.

- My necklace is too long – No one cares about how long your necklace is and if you had thought it was too long you would not have worn it in the first place. It is fine.

- My breath stinks – That is not possible because I had used breath mints already, so stop worrying about it.

- My butt is too fat for the seat – I am already in the seat, and we are already in the air. So it doesn't even matter anymore.

- I might have to pee – Solution: Just hold it!

- These people just brought me out of pity - A Fortune 500 company would not waste the time or money with someone on a plane for no reason. Besides that, I

GET OUT OF YOUR OWN WAY 5

know I add value and make a difference every time I go into a store.

- I don't really deserve to be here - You worked your way up from part-time seasonal help into a store manager and to the corporate office impacting hundreds of stores and you have also helped your team in the corporate office learn how to communicate to the stores with a recipe for success.

- My hair is not clean enough – You took a shower. Relax

- My fat rolls might be showing – Yep, and everyone else's are too!

- I wonder what my boss is thinking – Not your business.

- No one is talking, should I be talking? - No. Silence is okay.

This is such an important step in moving forward with your life. You have to really understand where and how you are sabotaging yourself. You have to start listening for it.

Pivotal Steps for Removing Negative Self-Talk

Step 1: Listen for your negative self-talk.

Step 2: Write it down & debunk it. Or if it is true, decide if it is something you can do anything about or not.

Step 3: Listen for it regularly so that you gain control of it.

Of course, this is just the stuff in your head that you never say out loud and maybe did not even realize that you were saying to yourself. You have had all this stuff in your head for so long that you are just used to it and have never confronted it. Sometimes to debunk or confront your self-talk you have to start identifying where it came from.

Example: In my negative self-talk I said I don't deserve to be here. I was told when I was young in my career that I could never be promoted because I did not have a college degree. I have been promoted several times since then and have made it to a very high level in the company.

GET OUT OF YOUR OWN WAY 7

However, that negative thought was still hanging out in the back of my head. At times, it was on top of my mind, and I did not even realize it.

Sometimes you have to dig a little deeper. If you feel like you cannot do that yourself then find someone to talk to.

Verbal Self-talk

There is also Verbal Self-talk. The kind you say out loud to make fun of yourself or negatively describe yourself.

"I am such a mess."

"I am a hot mess."

"I am never on time."

"I am fat."

STOP!!

Stop telling yourself and others that you are all these things. You are training your brain to believe them and in turn, inspiring more of them for yourself. It is amazing how hard we work to

8   MOVE

reach our goals and how much self-sabotage we work in along the way.

I was at lunch one day with an incredibly smart and talented woman. She had a degree in agriculture. She was enthusiastic about her business. She was 9 months pregnant and working on her business of renting chickens.

Yes, I said that she rents chickens for a living. We are in a café, and she is sitting across the table from me. She is glowing with that pregnancy glow. It is Monday and she is due Wednesday. She is explaining how she loves to watch the kids get so excited about her chickens and how their faces light up as they run over to them. Parents rent chickens from her for a couple of months, and she supplies the coop and the bedding, and everything they need to care for these chickens. She shares about her husband who is an engineer, and he is improving the chicken coop designs for her as well. She is so proud, and I am super inspired that someone could be so passionate about renting chickens. She then tells me that right now they have too

GET OUT OF YOUR OWN WAY 9

many eggs and wishes she could partner with a local bakery to use their farm-fresh eggs.

We then started talking about a nice little local bakery down the street and she was very excited about this idea. We were both happy we might have found her a solution.

Then it happens.

It was like watching the storm clouds roll in.

The shadow of doubt started to roll across her face and her expression turned dark.

She said, "I don't think we will be able to keep up with their demand."

I just stared at her. I was speechless for a moment. I could not even believe what had happened.

It was such an impressive display of self-sabotage.

WOW! Here was this amazing woman about to have her first baby in two days talking about her impressive chicken renting business and then she just talked herself out of moving forward.

10   MOVE

She convinced herself it would not work, in a matter of seconds.

But it isn't just her, is it? We all do that to ourselves now and then. So how do we stop? What makes us do that?

First, you have to understand that you do that to protect yourself. Sometimes it is because we have anxiety, low self-esteem, or depression, or it could be the environment in which we were raised. We feel insecure. We are not special or smart enough. If we don't put ourselves out there, we cannot get hurt or we won't fail. We naturally want to protect ourselves from things that are scary or different or unknown.

Let's talk about how we can stop.

Admit it when you do it.

I was getting my eyelashes filled and talking to my esthetician. We were talking about people putting themselves down. Ironically, I had been on the phone with her earlier and said, "I am a mess today."

GET OUT OF YOUR OWN WAY

After I got off the phone, I thought, that's not true. I am not a mess. I was just late.

You see, we were already committed to trying to get better at self-talk.

Anyway, she was always saying how much of a mess she is, and she says, "I am a hot mess."

So, in this conversation, I am telling her how I am trying not to give in to self-sabotage and get better with my self-talk.

She instantly says she knows a girl who says negative things about herself all the time.

I thought, "Well, you do it all the time, too." But I did not say that.

I just used my example of when I said it to her earlier.

Then she goes, "Well, does, 'I am a hot mess count?"

We both laughed. I said, "Yes!"

"Well, I guess I do it all the time too," she added.

My point is, you have to start watching for it to catch yourself doing it. You have to listen for your negative self-talk to creep in.

Pivotal Steps for Removing Negative Self-Talk

Step 1: Listen for your negative self-talk. Things you say to yourself and others. Listen to what you say about yourself out loud. What do you tell yourself you are not good at?

Example: "I am horrible at math." The reality is you are probably average. You can use a calculator on your phone just like everyone else unless you are still in school. No reason to even say that anymore.

Make a list of things that you have caught yourself saying you are bad at. Take a few minutes to write down all the things you can think of.

If you have a hard time catching yourself, start listening to what others say they are bad at, and write them down. This will help you know what you must be looking for.

GET OUT OF YOUR OWN WAY 13

Step 2: Write it down or say it out loud and then debunk it.

Things like "I am fat", "I am always late", and "I am always tired."

Okay, so now that you have made your list let's start debunking the things you say. Write down why those things are not right. Or if they have any truth to them, write down what you can do to change or fix them, so you feel better.

Step 3: Stop and correct yourself every time you start to self-sabotage.

For example:

Negative Self-talk: I am always late.
Self-correction: I am working on being on time.

Negative Self-talk: I am a mess.
Self-correction: I am organized, and I am juggling a lot of important things in my life.

Negative Self-talk: I am always broke.
Self-correction: I am paying all my bills and I have money for gas.

14   MOVE

All these things we are saying in our heads and out loud about ourselves control what we are or are not capable of. The more we are putting ourselves down, the more paralyzed in life we become. We can't move to the new house or get the new car or get the promotion we want or make the sales we want because we are taking it away from ourselves before we even have a chance. We are cutting ourselves off from opportunities in our lives.

Put yourself in a position to start moving toward what you want in life by quieting the negative self-talk and replacing it with either positive things about yourself or things in your life you are thankful for.

That is how you start getting out of your own way.

Chapter Two

Let it Go!

IF YOU ARE MAD, you are wasting your time! Yep, I said it. If you are angry, you are wasting your life. If you are sad, I am sorry, and you are wasting your brain power.

Now, I know that is not a very gentle way of putting things. Okay, it is super harsh. I know. When we get mad, sad, or hurt we just think about it over and over. We roll it around and imagine all these different outcomes. What we did or did not do. Sometimes we rewrite history to fit a better narrative. It does not matter. All that anger and frustration is taking up space and time in your life. It is sucking the life out of you to be angry, mad, or sad. No matter what, all the time we spend on feeding the anger becomes wasted time.

Things go wrong and sometimes we cannot change or fix anything. There are no right answers, and it is hard to even tell who or what to be mad at. The situation can get so frustrating that it consumes your brain. You dream about it. You wake up thinking about it. Within minutes of waking up, you can feel the anger bubbling in you. Your fists start to clinch, and you are so overwhelmed you don't know whether to cry or break something. Neither is a great answer.

You just keep replaying the situation over and over and maybe even rewiring your brain on what you said or how you handled it. None of it really matters, however. There is nothing you can do about what had happened. No matter how much you replay it in your head you cannot change the past. Most of the time you cannot understand or make any sense of what happened. You might try so hard to figure it out that it makes your head hurt.

MOVE

STOP! It's not going to work. You cannot rewrite it as you spin it in your brain a million times. You cannot change the past. It does not work that way. Quite possibly you cannot even make it hurt any less.

Have you ever heard the quote, "Holding onto anger is like drinking poison and expecting the other person to die." — **Gautama Buddha**.

I find that physical labor helps to get your brain working in the right direction. I also find that physical labor like pulling weeds also helps in parenting young teens. Anyway, that is for another book. You are learning in this book how important focusing your mind is for reaching your goals and moving yourself forward in life.

If you are focused on all the hurt and anger from your experiences, it makes it extremely hard to move at all. I say STOP thinking and start moving. I mean physically move. Go clean the garage or organize your closet. Go and make at least one square inch of space in your life better, cleaner, or more organized, literally! Then use that great feeling of accomplishment to lead your mind to move you forward.

When we reminisce over and over something we cannot change or fix we are using all that valuable space that makes the most important decisions in our life. We have things to do in our lives and the things we are supposed to do will help others as well. We have to find ways to get out of our own heads and do our part.

The examples I am using in this chapter might be much lighter than the pain or sadness you are dealing with in your life. Please understand I do not mean to diminish what you are going through.

Sally

Sally had a 25-year-old daughter. She and her daughter were close. Her daughter came over for dinner 2 nights a week and they spoke every day. Then one day her daughter decided she wanted space and did not want her mom in her life anymore. Sally was sad and heartbroken.

The bottom line is there is nothing Sally can do to change what her daughter wants. Sally can only control her own life. Sally cannot spend all of her time focused on what is or is not going on with her daughter. Her daughter is an adult and Sally, who is a really a great mom and a good person, has her own life to live.

Sally makes a significant difference in her community and several people around her are thankful for having her as a part of their lives. If Sally gets consumed with sadness not only does that stop Sally's life from moving forward but her community, friends, and family lose too.

Mark

Mark worked for a company for 5 years. He was very hopeful about getting promoted soon. He had made great sales and was making a significant impact on the company.

LET IT GO! 21

One day Mark came into work and his boss called him into his office.

Mark was excited! He thought this was about his great sales!

Mark's boss sat him down and told him the company was downsizing, and they were realigning his department.

Unfortunately, that meant Mark no longer had a position with the company.

Mark was so angry! He felt as though the people he trusted had turned their back on him!

He felt worthless. He was so confused. He kept thinking about what he could have and should have done.

The truth is it did not have anything to do with Mark. The owner of the company had made bad investments. Of course, Mark would never know that. All the days and weeks Mark spent rolling it all around in his head and being angry brought his life to a standstill. None of it was his fault. All the weeks he spent sad, angry, and letting the rest of his life go downhill, he was wasting time opening the door to better things.

Now please understand, if you are dealing with the loss of someone close to you then it might always hurt. One of the best ways to deal with the hurt is to move. I mean literally move. Get out of bed. Get out of the house. Force yourself to smile. It is a proven fact that the physical act of smiling starts to make you feel better even when it is fake. I am certainly not a counselor. If you absolutely cannot work through your emotions by yourself, you should get some kind of professional help. That could be a doctor, a counselor, or a life coach. This book is by no means meant to replace that kind of help or support.

What I am trying to get across is how to move forward in your life, to better your situation. You will have to let go of that hurt and anger to make room for positive thoughts that will start moving you in the right direction.

LET IT GO! 23

I am also not saying you should not be mad if someone has done you wrong. That anger is what will protect you from letting someone else do the same thing to you. But again, you are going to have to let go of some of it so you can move.

The thing about anger, frustration, and sadness is they make us feel powerless. They consume your brain so you cannot find solutions. The emotions make everything around you feel impossible. The negativity makes you feel worthless or believe there is no way out or there is no one to help you.

When I am hurt or angry about something major in my life, I have to tell myself, "Stop thinking about that person or situation. There is nothing I can do to change it. I need to focus on my life now and what I want to do."

Sometimes in the mornings, I have to wake up and make myself say what I am thankful for so that I don't go straight to what I am frustrated about.

Pivotal Steps to Help You Let Go and Make Room

Step 1: Acknowledge that it is consuming your brain.

This is an easy one. We usually know when something sad or angry is consuming our brains.

Step 2: Find the times of day or days of the week when it is the worst.

It is like when you are trying to lose weight. The doctor tells you to write down everything you eat. Make a note of when those thoughts are the worst. For me, it is in the morning. For you, it could be at night.

As you identify the worst times of the day or the worst days of the week you can start affecting them. Join a book club in the evening, go for a walk with your dog on the lake in the morning. Do something that makes you feel good during those times.

Step 3: Get moving. Add a new habit.

LET IT GO! 25

After you have found the worst times, you can replace those times with some kind of physical activity.

For example:

I am the worst in the morning when I have something sad or hurtful on my mind. I started going to the gym in the mornings. It forced my brain to figure out what I need to wear, what I need to take, and what I am going to do there.

This activity replaced all the other negative things that took that time and space. It also has the added benefit of being good for me.

I had more times during the day to fill up to change my mindset than just mornings. I joined a community service group, started singing lessons, joined self-defense classes including firearms training, and a kickball team. Actually, the list went on and on.

So, go clean the garage or organize your closet. Go and make a square inch of space in your life better, cleaner, or more organized.

Step 4: Take a deep breath and think of the things you are thankful for or the positive things or people in your life.

There are entire books on just this topic and if you need support with letting go of anger or sadness talk with a professional. Get yourself the help you need. Once you get some help and start letting go, 6 months from now you won't believe how much your life will have changed. You need that space and brain power.

Chapter Three

The Big F's

Failure

I love to imagine a picture of me falling with my face planted into the snow. It is cold and it kind of hurts. I don't like it, but I am okay. I call it falling forward.

When I was in my early 20's I was stubborn and had a big ego, especially about being able to keep up with my 3 brothers. They thought we should all go skiing. We lived in a town almost on a mountain so instead of playing football we went skiing. On the way up to the mountain my brother Lance, who was close to my age, convinced me and my youngest brother Landon that we should snowboard instead of ski because it was so much more fun. Our oldest brother Chuck who was about 10 years older than me was not having it. He was insistent to stay on skis. When we got there me, my two brothers, and their friend all got snowboards and headed up to the top of the mountain.

We got to the top of the mountain and asked Lance, "How does this work?"

He looked at all of us with our snowboards and said, "I don't really know I have only done it once."

Then he took off on his boards down the mountain. Well, at that point the only way to really get down the mountain is to go. So that is what we did. After one hot minute, I was planted face down in the snow with a snowboard strapped to my boots and had no idea how to use it. Still close to the top. I got mad and tried to turn it over. I did not consider that my feet were locked in place and as I flipped over, I heard a crack in my ankle and instantly felt pain.

30   MOVE

I was so mad. I sat there and cried for a minute and then realized there was no one else around me and I was sitting on a mountain of snow by myself and somehow still had to get down the mountain. That was pathetic and certainly not keeping up with the boys

There were not many options for getting off that mountain. All I could think was how I was not going to be the girl that got hurt right away. My brothers would never let me live it down and would not let me go next time. I tightened my boot up and decided I was going to do what I could to figure out how to get down. I slid on my butt for a little while but that was taking forever, and I did not have that much patience. So, I braved standing on my board again and started sliding. It was much faster than sliding on my ass down the mountain. I continued to fall, get up, and snowboard a little farther and faster each time. I had a few flickering moments where I felt like I might actually be snowboarding.

At some point, I had made it all the way back down to the lodge that had a bar. I found my oldest brother there as well. I did not tell him I had gotten hurt, I just sat down and ordered a Jack and Coke.

Turns out it had only been about an hour, and we had the rest of the day before the other boys would be done. I did not want to sit there all day so back up the mountain I went. I spent the next 5 hours snowboarding. I ran into my brothers on the mountain a few times and overall had a good day. It was the day prior to New Year's Eve and I had sprained my ankle so once I took off the boot I could not really walk or bear any weight and my boyfriend had to carry me into the bar on New year's eve.

We all mess up. Especially as we learn new things, we mess up even more. We all get it wrong quite often.

I used to tell my employees, "If you are not messing anything up, you are not doing enough."

You learn your most valuable lessons by messing up.

Did you know that JK Rowling was rejected by 12 publishers before someone accepted Harry

Potter? Now they say her net worth is over 1 billion dollars.

The interesting thing about failure is it opens other doors for us. We learn things and we meet people. We are able to tell our stories in a way that relates to others. Our experiences make us special. You cannot let just one thing decide your self-worth or success. You have to look at the bigger picture.

When I was a co-Store Manager for a big-box retail store, I helped solve several problems in stores in Tulsa, Oklahoma. I did such a great job that I got promoted to the market team.

My job was to oversee the Tire and Lube express areas of 11 stores in the market. I enjoyed my job. I was about 4 months into the position, and I was making a real difference. We had a great market team and I respected them.

One night they called our entire team and told all of us we could not come to the office until 10 am the next morning. The next morning a couple of us went for breakfast while we were waiting. There was a real sadness in the air. We were all afraid that we were going to lose our jobs. Well, the others were.

I was sure that could not really happen. I had worked for this company for 10 years and I had done amazing things and moved my family across the country from Spokane, Washington to Tulsa, Oklahoma. We had built a house there and we believed we were living the dream. I was working with the smartest people I had ever met. They were all so talented and I felt lucky to be part of this team. There was just no way the company would let go of such great talent.

We finished breakfast and went to the office and one by one we were sat down and told we no longer had our jobs.

We had to turn in our company laptops and our company cars, and another dagger was when they asked for my name badge. It said 10 years and had my pins and things I had collected over time. It was like a part of me that was being taken away. I felt my eyes grow big as I was in disbelief. It was like I was watching a movie from the outside because it was so unbelievable.

34   MOVE

We would still be employed for a couple of months to try to find something else in the company but as of now, we cannot come back to the office. 10 years of exemplary service and that was it. I am not sure there are words to describe how I felt. I had tears welling up in my eyes, but I refused to cry. I was not giving anyone the satisfaction of seeing me cry. I could feel the pain in my stomach and my fist was clenched as if to give me strength. I was escorted out of the building; they explained it was just policy. I am sure you can imagine the things I was feeling. I was torn between feeling I was worthless and disposable to being mad at the company to being sad it was someone on our team who had been chosen to give each of us this horrible news.

As I was adjusting mentally to what happened and working to get back on my feet someone gave me this piece of advice that stuck with me.

He took a $20 bill out of his pocket and said, "What is this?"

"It is a $20 bill," I replied, short and irritated at him for asking me such a stupid question.

Then he crumpled it up and threw it on the ground and then stepped on it and smashed it into the dirt. He rubbed it around really good. Then he picked it up and straightened it back out and asked, "What is it now?"

"Ahhh......." My eyebrows raised, and I cracked a partial smile. I felt relief come over me as I replied, "Still a $20 bill."

WOW!

He said, "Windy, people can use you and crumple you up and even throw you in the garbage, but you are still a $20 bill. Don't ever forget that."

It was amazing how those 5 minutes all of a sudden made me feel like I was worth something again.

I share this story with you because we all fail all the time. It is part of life. How we manage our failures is what really matters. It is about remembering that you are always falling forward. Even if you failed this time, you know more than you did last time. Don't let yourself ruminate over your failures or shortcomings.

36   MOVE

Tell yourself how awesome you are and keep going. Continue moving ahead with the same confidence you started with. Well, it would make sense to have the same confidence or even more because you are smarter now.

I read a book on salary negotiation, and I was determined that in my next evaluation meeting with my boss, I was going to try it. I got myself all bold and geared up and asked for what I wanted and had solid reasons why. I presented the evidence of my work and why I was worth it. All was good until my boss said, "That is more than I make!"

I hadn't taken that into account.

Epic Fail!

That was okay. I learned I need to get an understanding of how much they are willing to give me so that my ask can be successful. Obviously, my boss would not give me a raise more than her pay but if I had been in the range between us, I might have got it. After that lesson, I was able to secure a few good pay negotiations. Also, I learned that sometimes they

THE BIG F'S 37

won't negotiate in pay but in other perks like relocation packages and paid time off.

The next time the company asked me to relocate and I had taken the salary negotiation as far as it could go, I moved on to perks like my relocation package. I was a bottom-tier relocation and there were 3 tiers, so I printed the top tier and mine and made a list of the things the top tier received that I did not. You see they had a lot more room on the relocation perks. I received all of the perks I asked for.

You have to fail to succeed but if you don't do anything you won't get anything.

You have to pick yourself up and dust yourself off and move on. I know that is easier said than done. People say guys are better about this than women and sometimes that is true.

Sometimes it is easier if you use an example. Do you know a person who messes up often and is not bothered by that?

That person is a great example.

I like to use the analogy in my head to let it roll off my back. I actually picture a big ball and my back is arched over and it is rolling down. That sounds kind of silly, but it works for me.

I also say things to myself like, "That's how you learn."

Or sometimes I get pissed off and then I put my brain to work on figuring out how to do it differently.

I had to fail to learn more and go on to be successful.

Henry Ford is one of my favorites because we still have, drive, and buy Ford vehicles. And, he did not even have much formal education!

"Failure is simply the opportunity to begin again, this time more intelligently." – Henry A. Ford ("Failing for Success: Henry A. Ford | Intellectual Ventures")

Henry Ford's first two automotive companies failed. The board of directors dissolved the first one and he left the second due to differences. Two different companies failing. Now that's pressure! It would be hard to start a 3rd company after that. I mean it would be impossible if all you did was sit around and sulk about your failure. We are all better off because he started his 3rd company. It is still affecting people's lives a hundred years later.

Thomas Edison's is another great story about failure.

"I haven't failed, I have just found 1000 ways that won't work." – Thomas A. Edison

His teachers thought he was stupid, and he got fired from his first couple of jobs. He saw lots of failures. Yet he ended up inventing the electric light bulb, the phonograph, batteries, and many more things that still affect our way of living today.

We have to fail. We have to fall down. We have to miss the goal. We need failure just as much as we need success. Just like you need to be happy and sad. You cannot really appreciate winning if you have never lost.

40   MOVE

My son was 8 years old, and he said "Mom, I wish everyday was Christmas."

Wow!

Could you even imagine if every day was Christmas? You would be tired of opening presents. It would not be special.

He might then be wishing, "Can't we just have one day with no Christmas?"

Christmas happening only once a year is what makes it special.

Also, we learn more from our failures than we do from our successes. Failure is part of the process. It is a part of the journey!

It's how we learn to get better. It's how we make each other better. You have value to bring to this world. You matter to the people around you and you might matter to generations after you.

Winston Churchill once said, "Success is not final, Failure is not fatal; it is the courage to continue that counts."

Fear

Let's talk about the other big F word – Fear.

Fear can be paralyzing. It can make you remain in unhealthy situations at work or in relationships.

I always tell my kids, "Be afraid but don't let it stop you."

I say that because I think a little fear is good. It pushes you to do better, be more prepared, and get more help. When your fear gets to a point that it is stopping you from moving from the situation then it is not good anymore.

When I was in my early 20s I was a single mom. I worked for a big-box retailer as an hourly manager and had for a couple of years. I really wanted to be promoted to a salaried manager, but I was afraid to speak up and tell anyone. I just went on for almost another year doing the same job wishing in my head I could be promoted but too afraid to do anything about it. Not only was that not good for me but it was not giving my daughter my best either.

42 MOVE

Finally, one day I got the nerve and went to my market manager. I told him I wanted to be a Salaried Manager. He said the next week he would send me on a trial run and see how it goes. He sent me to another town to do a store remodel. That was where I met my husband by the way. I did great there and in the next two months, I was promoted. As a matter of fact, I did such a great job that they started me at about $6,000 a year, higher than the other managers. I had let fear stop me for a long time.

I decided I was going to work on not letting my fear stop me from speaking up anymore.

I use another trick I learned in my Dale Carnegie Training. They teach you to ask yourself, "What is the worst that can happen?" Once you answer that, then accept and prepare for that. Plan for how to manage the worst that can happen. Then things tend to seem less scary. The reality is it seldom goes to the worst-case scenario.

Don't be afraid to fail. Don't let it discourage you. There are so many times when I dig inside myself to figure out why I am not doing something and realize it is because I am afraid of failing.

Pivotal Steps for Dealing with Fear and Failure

Step 1: Make a list of things in which you feel like you have failed. Think through situations that did not work out.

Step 2: Now take each of those things and write down what you learned. How you would do it differently next time? Was there a positive outcome? Did something happen that you are thankful for in your life?

Step 3: Take the time to think through what you are afraid might happen if you try again or move in a situation. Sometimes just writing this makes these things seem less scary.

STEP 4: "Be afraid but don't let it stop you." Accept and prepare for the worst then move forward. Write down what you are afraid of and what you are going to do that is good for you. How is that going to move your life forward?

Chapter Four

Step by Step Walking Out of Overwhelm

Overwhelmed! "I am so overwhelmed." It is like once we learned that word, we could just say it and then…. nothing.

The word itself literally means "Bury or drown beneath a huge mass."

We all have times when we get overwhelmed.

There are so many reasons why we feel overwhelmed. Work, life changes, moving, new jobs, new bosses, school, family changes, loss of someone you love to distance or relationship, social obligations, or just life in general. We all feel overwhelmed, anxious, or stressed at some point. When you are feeling overwhelmed give yourself a break and be kind to yourself.

There is a normal number of things we can manage. When things change, they can put us into a space where we no longer have enough time or energy to manage all the pieces.

I am going to share some steps to help you work yourself out of being overwhelmed and get you moving forward in your life. If you struggle to work out of your overwhelm even after consciously making an effort, you might need more help or support with what you are going through. That is okay and I encourage you to seek the extra support you need. Get a counselor or find a professional to talk to.

You matter and helping you move forward in your life will make all our lives better.

You usually know you are overwhelmed because you are frustrated or mad or just don't care.

Okay, but what do we do with it?

STEP BY STEP WALKING OUT OF... 47

Being overwhelmed is a problem and once you are overwhelmed you cannot move or do anything. You are at a standstill.

Take a deep breath.

Picture yourself as a stick person and you have a circle drawn around you. It is like you are in the middle of this circle and there is no way out. Now picture your stick figure reaching up to the circle and cutting the cord with a pair of scissors and then laying that cord out in a straight line in front of you. Now you have a path forward.

To get yourself out of overwhelm you must start by cutting the cord of that circle. And it won't be a circle anymore. Lay it in a straight line to create a path you can follow.

Take a minute to just picture that.

Okay so how do we do that? It sounds easy but, doing it, that is another story. You have to start somewhere. Like where did the stick person get the scissors to cut the cord? You must have something to give you the ability to cut the cord of the circle.

You Start by Making a List

Your list is what gives you the ability to cut the cord and start down a path.

You can do it on your phone or on paper. It does not matter if it is digital or physical. If you are reading a physical copy of this book, you have a note page exactly for that purpose.

Make a list and put everything that comes into your brain on the list. I mean all of it. We can cross stuff off later. At this moment take out your pen and paper or your phone or your laptop or tablet and start writing. I mean everything! Feed the dog. Take kids to school. Return a phone call. Return 20 phone calls. Note each call and who it is to on an individual item on the list. Every place you need to go. Mom's birthday gift. All of it! Do not leave a single thing off your list, no matter how small.

All the things on your mind, from small to big, personal, and professional. All the things that are in your brain. It is kind of a brain dump.

STEP BY STEP WALKING OUT OF...

Once you have everything written down, breathe and take a break.

Yes, go take a break. If you think that you can't afford a break because you have too much to do, then just remember that while you are overwhelmed you are not getting anything done anyway.

Take a deep breath. Do breathing exercises. If you do meditation, take 10 minutes and do that. Do yoga, or take your dog on a walk. Watch a short TV show that makes you laugh or feel good. Do something to completely take your mind off your list and all the stuff you have to do or the guilt of what you are not getting done. Go watch the panda cam at the zoo or watch cat videos online. Give yourself a breather.

I like to write my big list before bed and leave it on my night stand. It helps me sleep better because I know I don't have to think about it and I can clear my brain and won't forget anything. Sometimes I will make my list and then go watch TV for 30 minutes and get a drink and a snack, then come back to it.

50   MOVE

A few minutes to be "off the hook" so to speak.

Then come back to your list. The list is like taking the scissors and cutting the cord on the circle. The list is how you will lay out a path forward.

Take a good look at this big list you made and first be proud of yourself.

WOW! Nice work!

- Now you have this huge list of everything on your mind.

- You have taken the scissors and cut the cord on the circle and stopped turning.

- You have taken the first step to build your path.

Okay now, let's be real. There is no possible way one person could get all these things done in one day! No way!

Even if you were Superman, it would not happen!

Cut yourself some slack and give yourself some credit.

Working the List

There are things you can do that are easy.

Find the 5 easiest things and go get them done and off the list.

It is important to be able to see your progress. I like to highlight the stuff I have done so I can still see it. Doing the easiest things on the list first is like laying out the path. It motivates you. It gets you moving. It makes your brain start focusing in one direction.

Laying Your Path = Organizing Your List

Now for the Journey down the path. One foot in front of the other.

Take your list and prioritize it. This might take a little time.

Write down the things that have due dates or time limits — I have a meeting at 1 p.m. Kids need to be picked up at 3 p.m.

Then work on other things around it — I can call the vet for my dog while I am waiting in line to pick up the kids.

This is how you start laying out your path.

Time Management

Write next to each item how long each thing takes.

- It takes 3 hours to make a slide deck.

- To clean my kitchen, I can get a lot done in 45 minutes.

- It will take 2 hours to get the reports together for my boss.

Then do the easiest thing that takes the least time first. Once you start crossing stuff off your list you will start feeling better and you will be able to breathe, and you will find that you are starting to be productive. It will feel like you are following your path to success.

As you continue prioritizing you will quickly identify if might need help. You will also see things that can be done together or in the same time frame.

STEP BY STEP WALKING OUT OF...

Say "No" nicely

Are there things you could say "NO" to?

Your time is valuable.

- It is your job to protect your time.

- It is your right to protect your time.

- You can say no kindly.

For many of us the word 'No' is packed with guilt, and we are afraid someone will be disappointed or maybe we won't ever get that opportunity again. Learning how to say no is an important part of keeping control and using our time wisely. After all, you cannot do everything.

Here are some great ways to say no.

"Now is not a great time for me."

"I wish I could, but I am covered up."

"I don't have the bandwidth right now."

"I have another commitment."

54   MOVE

"Let me know next time."

"My schedule is full for the next couple of weeks. Can we try after that?"

It is also okay to go back to someone and say, "I know I said I would do this, but I can't right now. I am sorry."

They might be disappointed, but chances are you will feel much better after. The reality is they will get over it.

I am part of a community outreach group and I have a good friend who is the president of the group. He has asked me to be the next president. It was a nice honor to be asked but I did not want to do that. Nothing in me really wanted to be the president. I had other priorities in my life. My son was graduating high school the next year and I had other stuff going that I preferred to spend my time doing. I felt bad telling him no, but it was important that I did what was right for me and my life.

It is okay to say no. It does not make you weak. As a matter of fact, it makes you stronger and more motivated when you have more control over your schedule.

With all that: Is there anything on your list that you need to say no to? Do you need to go back to anyone and let them know you will not be able to do something? It is hard to do but you will be relieved once it is done.

Share the Load / Get Help

Ask, "Who else can help me with the things on this list?"

A great question.

Is there someone you can share your list with that will help you prioritize or can take things off the list for you? Maybe it's a coworker who can help you make a few calls. Or maybe your spouse can help. I know sometimes when I share my list with my husband, he will offer to do a few things.

At home can your husband, wife, son, or daughter feed the dog, do a load of dishes, or switch the laundry.

Can you break the tasks down into pieces so others can help you? Maybe you need to clean the fridge. Can everyone in the house take one shelf? Maybe you will pay someone else to come clean your fridge and take it off your list completely. There might be someone around you that can help.

Showing someone else your massive list or being vulnerable and asking for help can sometimes be an uncomfortable feeling. And, back to all the stuff we already discussed about self-talk!

Repeat to yourself that all those feelings crowding in your head are OKAY. It is okay to ask for help and it is good to receive help. Others give you strength. Share your list with others around you. Others will have ideas of ways to help, or they might have time or resources you did not think of.

Let's be honest. It is hard to think of solutions when you are overwhelmed.

As you are laying out your path, you will also be working on your list.

STEP BY STEP WALKING OUT OF... 57

Now that you have prioritized, organized, managed your time, said "No", and asked for help, keep working on your list. You are on a roll and no longer stuck. Keep up the good work.

When you find yourself spinning in that circle of overwhelm, cut the cord, lay out a path, and start walking down your path step-by-step to success.

Prevent Overwhelm. Stay Organized.

Now let's talk about some solutions to prevent this from happening again. Here is one of my biggest secrets to keeping myself from getting overwhelmed.

Staying Organized

Suppose you receive emails and phone calls all day long and cannot get anything done. You need to find a way to block out some time for projects and to complete work.

It can look something like this.

In the morning block out 2 hours when you do not respond to any emails or phone calls or messages and only work on projects. Say 9-11 am. Then, at 11.01 check all your messages and take care of things.

I used to work in a job where I would get close to 300 emails a day. Of course, there was no way to get anything else done if I only focused on those, but I had lots of other responsibilities. So I read my emails first thing in the morning, before lunch at 2 pm and at 4:30 pm.

I set up folders for automated emails which I could read later and scheduled time to read them weekly. I had emails from my boss come in highlighted so I could differentiate them. I set times my phone went to voicemail especially the week the monthly number came out.

I broke my month into weekly focus projects. I did monthly training videos and monthly profit and loss reviews. I worked on projects the week prior to their due dates.

You are going to have days that throw a wrench in your plans but that is okay. Just start again tomorrow.

Schedule Yourself Some "Me" time

You need to do something that makes you feel good about yourself. You need a little time outside your daily life.

Something that helps me is going to the gym before work. I go to the gym for 1 hour each morning Monday-Thursday, and I set out my clothes for the whole week on Sunday so I can just fall out of bed and get into my gym clothes.

Work to plan out your calendar in advance. Block time for specific things. It is not always going to work out but the times it does will put you ahead of the game.

It is not just about organizing your time. You also have to do a little self-assessment.

Self-assessment

I feel more focused when reading early in the morning. I am better at talking to people in the afternoon. If I have meetings I need to present or speak at, I schedule them in the afternoons. The ones I can just listen to or read as emails, I keep them for the mornings. For example, when

I proofread chapters of this book I did it in the mornings.

I was born and brought up on the West Coast on Pacific Time, and even though I have lived in the Central Time Zone for 15 years my brain still works on Pacific Time. So, I try never to take meetings or talk to people before 9 a.m. Central. Because my brain thinks it is before 7 a.m. and refuses to get ready for a conversation. Plus, I tend to be short-tempered and come across in a less positive manner.

As you organize your time and start planning ahead, you will feel more prepared and more in control. That confidence will help you protect your time. Politely say "No" to things that will overwhelm your schedule. As you start getting into a routine, people around you will get to know your schedule and support you.

Pivotal Steps for Overwhelm

Step 1: Acknowledging that you are overwhelmed. Taking the time to breathe and maybe cry if that is what you need. Realize you are running in a circle and no longer moving.

STEP BY STEP WALKING OUT OF...

Step 2: Make a list. Dump your brain. Put it all down where you can see it. On paper, on your phone, on your computer, on a dry-erase board. Put everything on the list. Put all your personal and professional things on the list.

Step 3: Work on your list.

- Do easy, quick things to start you in the right direction and cross them off.

- Prioritize and organize your list.

- Say no to the unnecessary things on your list.

- Continue working on your list until it is so messy from stuff crossed out that you have to make a new one or don't need one at all.

Step 4: Ask for help. Share your list with someone else. Get support. If needed, get professional support.

Step 5: Organize your time. Block time in your schedule to take steps for prevention.

Chapter Five

Attitude Is Everything

IT IS YOUR JOB to Choose Your Attitude!

My hair stylist was doing my hair while telling me how horrible she was at using technology.

She said, "I am terrible at all that new stuff."

I said with a smile, "With an attitude like that, I am sure."

She said, "You know what, you are right."

The new stuff she was talking about was Facebook and it had been around for 18 years by then.

64   MOVE

Every time you tell yourself you cannot do something, or you are not good at something you are just making things harder. You are the only one who can choose your attitude. As a matter of fact, it is your job to choose your attitude. We can blame others and we can come up with lots of reasons why it is someone else's fault that we are sad or miserable or we cannot move our lives forward. But the truth is, we have the power to choose our attitude.

I have a fabulous friend. She is about 4.5 feet tall and has the biggest smile you have ever seen. She is always upbeat, saying things like, "Come on, let's do it."

She always wants to share everything and bring joy to others despite going through numerous tragedies in recent years. One day she texted me that a big storm had washed out her road to the lake. I thought, "Wow, that was going to be so much work to fix, and it was going to be so expensive".

Her next text was about how blessed she was in her life to have a road to the lake be washed

ATTITUDE IS EVERYTHING 65

out. This had always been her dream to have this great property with lake access to fish. She decided to have an attitude of gratefulness about the whole incident.

Choosing to be thankful for things in your life can help foster a positive attitude. Thankfulness, by definition, is the feeling of being happy or grateful because of something.

When I was a young adult, my first car was an old, stick-shift Mustang that my older sister had wrecked. It was not a cool Mustang; it did not have much of the driver's seat left. I had to stop every now and then and refill the oil and put water in the radiator. The door had about half an inch between the door frame and the car. It would rain and snow inside the car and the windshield was cracked. Then I got a cream-colored Ford Taurus. It would have been described as an old lady car. Back in the '90s that was not a very desirable car. But I was thankful that I had a car that stayed dry in the rain and snow. I could see out my windshield; watching my windshield wipers at work felt like magic. The view from the window would instantly fill me up.

I was thankful for the driver's seat. I was thankful for how safe I felt in my new car. I did not have to carry extra oil or jugs of water to get around town. My new car may not have been a big deal to someone else, but I was thankful for it.

We all have things and people around us to be thankful for. There are several books on how being grateful can make a positive impact on your life.

These days I am thankful that I have been smart enough to hold on to my amazing husband when I was young and making stupid decisions. I am thankful for my little pug that loves me no matter what. I am thankful for the great mattress on my bed because it is so comfortable.

Look around you right now and make a mental list of the things for which you have to be grateful. I am not saying that you will not have pain over terrible things that have happened in your life. Of course, those pains will still be there. But when you focus on the things you are thankful for, your feelings will improve.

ATTITUDE IS EVERYTHING

Your attitude towards the world will change positively.

I feel like it could be an unwritten rule that when I am getting ready for a big day something will go wrong. I almost always spill coffee somewhere and I forget something. So, years ago, I started a new attitude. So now when my coffee spills as I am getting out of my car, I say, "Okay, now I am going to have a great day because something bad has already happened."

It tricks my brain into believing that now everything will be great.

You know what? It works every time. Sometimes I am like, "I am glad that this mess was easy to clean up."

Sometimes when my coffee spills and hardly makes any mess I am so excited because I got my bad thing out of the way, and it was not even that bad. With a little time and practice, you can very successfully adopt a different attitude toward hard things in life.

You have to catch yourself and start asking how you can turn it around. Then you have to start taking the time to actually turn it around whether you say it out loud or not.

When you find yourself frustrated or angry because something has unexpectedly ruined your day, how can you turn that around? How can you make that bad thing into something positive? Sometimes shifting your perspective can help you find the silver lining. Recollect the past when you still managed to have a good day despite your difficulties. There is always something, you just have to find it. Remember, it is your job to control your attitude.

Guilt

Our guilt has an interesting way of taking over our moods and actions. We all feel guilty about things we have not done. We accumulate all this guilt inside our brains and take it out on others to make ourselves feel better. Or we overreact to a situation because we feel guilty about something else. I find that as a mother of young adults I have spent a lot of time in my children's life feeling guilty about things that they don't remember or did not matter to them.

I tell you this because being aware of how your guilt negatively affects your attitude can help you adjust. Also, the negativity you receive from someone could be completely based on their own guilt and issues and most probably has nothing to do with you at all.

Let's get to the biggest, simplest, most impactful way to adjust your attitude and positively impact others.

Smiles Matter

Let me tell you about how I learned to smile. Early in my career at a Fortune 500 company, I was a very diligent worker and continuously received recognition. I was young, motivated, and I could work more pallets of freight in one night than most people. I prided myself on how much I was able to do physically. One of the things that made me so efficient was that I did not like talking to others. I did not want to know about their families. I did not want to know their life stories. Mostly because I did not want to share my own. I had grown up with a very sordid past. I didn't really have a mom and dad to talk about. How many siblings I have was a hard question to answer. I just wanted everyone to leave me alone and get to work.

As I continued to grow with the company, I was promoted to an hourly supervisor managing others. To tell you the truth I shouldn't have been managing anyone. I wasn't very friendly. I didn't have compassion. I was usually angry.

As I continued to grow, they started telling me things like, "You should smile once in a while," or "You should let the associates win now and then." Then I had a supervisor who recommended that I read the book "How To Win Friends and Influence People" by Dale Carnegie. He told me that he really felt like the advice in that book can help me.

If you meet me today, you wouldn't even know that I had to learn how to smile. There's a chapter in that book that does nothing but teach you how to smile. When I was young in my management career, I really wanted to be better, so I worked on

ATTITUDE IS EVERYTHING

it. It was not normal for me to smile. It was not comfortable. My face felt like it did not belong to that shape. I would drive to work, get out of my car, stand next to it, take a deep breath, and put a smile on my face that was very fake. Then I would hold my smile on my face all the way through the parking lot and all the way to the back of the store until I got to the office where I felt like I could breathe.

I had mixed feelings about this. I didn't want to be fake. I have never liked people who were fake. I learned very quickly that if you smile at others, they smile back at you.

There is something about the popular saying "Fake it until you make it!"

Before I knew it, I was smiling at people, and they were smiling back at me. It was like a whole new feeling. I was enjoying the smiles that people gave to me. It made a difference in how I felt. After months of training myself and all the wonderful smiles that others shared with me, my smile was not fake anymore.

When you smile it makes you feel better, and it is contagious.

It Is Not Always About You!

This makes a big difference for me. I know it is hard to believe that the obnoxiousness that you receive from someone else is not about you.

Once I started realizing how other people act is not always about me, getting through my day became easier. It may sound arrogant, but the reality is that we often take inspiration from others and base our reactions on how their actions make us feel. Of course, if someone makes a foolish decision, the consequences are their own responsibility. However, in general, most people tend to focus on themselves and their own lives, and others' actions may simply be an interruption to their thoughts about themselves.

Suppose your co-worker has a harsh tone. Well, they could be having a bad day. They could be having issues with their significant other. Their mom or dad might be sick. Their kids could be acting out and getting kicked out of school. Their

ATTITUDE IS EVERYTHING

attitude toward you is not always about you. It mostly has to do with them.

So, at times, it is helpful to remind yourself that it is not about you.

I wish I had been able to do this when I was younger. I had a boss who treated me poorly, constantly criticizing and belittling me. She only had mean things to say. I was miserable and consumed by her negativity toward me. But, what I did not understand at the time was that her mom was dying of cancer. Her mother was her closest friend, and her mother's death was the most devastating thing she had ever experienced. I was merely an inconvenience to her during that difficult time.

For a full year of my career, I was paralyzed by all the negativity and consumed by it. It does not make how she treated me right but what I let it do to me would have been different if I had adopted this attitude sooner.

So, that person being rude to you is not your problem! Now, how great is that? Love it when it is not my problem!

Make a "Great Job" Folder!

When you feel that others value you or appreciate you it makes you feel better. It fills you up.

How do you find it when you need it?

Something a good friend of mine taught me is to keep a 'Good job' folder. This friend of mine is one of the smartest, most talented people I have ever met. He is always the smartest person in the room, and he is very humble so sometimes people don't even know it. He genuinely cares about people and is always calm and on point. He is truly amazing. Who would ever think someone like that would ever feel down or have self-doubt. He taught me a valuable trick that helps him when his self-doubt sneaks in and he is feeling down.

He keeps a 'Good job' folder.

"What is that?" you ask.

He collects notes and letters of appreciation that others send him or give him, and he keeps them in a folder. If his boss sends him a compliment or

ATTITUDE IS EVERYTHING

a coworker sends a nice message or if someone sends him a card, they go to his folder. He keeps all those things so he can go back and review them.

It is human nature to focus on the bad. We let the good things flow like water right through our brains but when something bad happens we hold on to it tight and go round and round with it. We obsess over it and sometimes that is the only thing we remember.

If you have a good job file, you can refer to it when things are hard. When you need an attitude adjustment, refer to those nice things people said about you. Read a thank you card or a congratulatory note; a memory of anything you did that made someone else's day.

Create a folder, digital or physical, and save the 'good job' mementos. File it when someone emails you a thank you note or tells you did a great job at something. Once a month or once a week read all the nice things people have said about you. That way we learn to cherish the good, too.

MOVE

Positive Attitude Strategies

There is one strategy I use to keep a positive attitude. I keep a digital calendar and my goal is always to have a badass day. Inspired by the book, "You Are a Badass" by Jen Sincero. Each day I add notes about the day to my calendar and the word WIN in big letters. So, I can see each day that I accomplished my goals and won.

When you feel good about yourself it is always easier to go out into the world with a positive attitude.

There are lots of different ways to get help with this. Think through who you are and what is meaningful to you.

- You can get apps for inspirational messages or a calendar with positive quotes.

- Go through all the things you are thankful for.

- Think of the people in your life whom you are thankful for. I have the habit of sending little messages telling my dear ones the specific things I appreciate about them.

- Meditation can be helpful for clearing your mind and adjusting your attitude.

- Foods like ice cream can adjust your attitude. You know the famous "Need a Snickers bar" commercial. There is a reason that the commercial is relatable.

- If you have a spiritual relationship, take time for prayer. That is a great way to help you get to a positive place and get your attitude moving in a positive direction.

- Ask for help. If you are having trouble finding your way to a positive place or feel like you cannot get there on your own, ask for help. Find trained professionals who can help you change your attitude and situation. It could be a medical professional, counselor, or therapist.

MOVE

Pivotal Steps to Attain Your Best Attitude

Step 1: Make and keep a 'Thankful Journal'. I know that sounds a little hooey, but it really helps. Every day make a list of the things you are thankful for. That will help you identify the people and things around you that you have to appreciate. Use these things to be grateful.

Step 2: Pay attention to the things that make you mad, frustrated, or angry and think of ways to make them positive.

Step 3: Smile, even if it is fake. Fake it till you make it.

Step 4: Make a digital or physical 'good job' folder. Schedule time once a week/month to read through it.

Remember, it is not always about you!

Chapter Six

Lifting the Weight

Moving forward is the only way to leave the past behind.

Ask For Help

It takes humility to admit you need help and it requires great courage to ask someone for help. We live in a society that constantly professes the idea of being independent and strong, and not needing help from anyone.

Humans are social beings. If you find that, despite working through these tips and tricks you cannot adjust your thinking to a positive light, move yourself forward and ask for help.

To help literally means, making it easier for someone to do something by offering one's services or resources. Allow someone to make it easier for you.

There are lots of self-sabotaging reasons why we don't ask for help. For me, I have trust issues and deep down I feel like if I ask for help then that gives someone some kind of leverage to hold over me or to use against me later.

- You might feel that asking for help makes you weak.

- You might imagine that requesting help means becoming a burden to someone.

- You might have convinced yourself that no one wants to help you, or no one can, so you just need to do it yourself.

- Or maybe (this notion has been very hard for me to work on) after you ask for help, receiving help is uncomfortable.

It's okay. It is okay to ask for help. Asking for help makes you stronger. No one who has ever made big things happen, did it alone. They have always had help. As human beings, we all require assistance at some point in our lives, without exception.

Visibility From the Outside

If you are experiencing feelings of confusion or have gone through a traumatic event, or if someone close to you is going through a difficult time, seeking external assistance may be beneficial. Having someone who fully supports you can make it easier to move forward. This help is not meant to be permanent, just a temporary aid until you begin to feel better. Think of using it as a crutch until you can walk on your own.

It is often easier to see a clear direction from an outside perspective. This is why people say that hindsight is 20/20.

Think of yourself in a snow globe. You are in a ball and snow is falling all around. Your visibility is not good. You get all caught up in what is all around you and can't see a clear path. You have all the emotions, self-driven guilt, and several reasons to justify your feelings. Your vision nears zero at times. But if you are on the outside, it is much clearer.

Sometimes you need someone on the outside to help you get out of the snow globe and get you on The Yellow Brick Road. A path you can follow to move forward in your life. Someone to hear your story and help you work through the hurts burdening you.

Life is difficult and we have times when we need someone to journey with us. If you have free resources like companies offering free counseling, make use of them. Or spend the money to pay someone to help you. That could be a counselor or a life coach or an executive coach or a business coach.

Find someone who is an expert on your specific subject. For example, if you're working on marriage issues then seek a marriage counselor. If it is business related, get a business coach. If it is anxiety, self-esteem, or depression, talk to your doctor or find a counselor that specializes in that subject.

The wonderful thing about all these people is that whoever you choose, they will have your best interest in mind. The professional will always handle your feelings with care and help you broaden your perspective to see your story in a more optimistic light. They will not be judgmental as you open up about your past mistakes. A slight shift in perspective can have a significant impact on your understanding and how to work through the issues at hand.

We need to get over the shame in asking for help. Do not give in to the popular misconception that asking for help or talking to someone about your problems makes you weak or a failure. The only way we really fail is by doing nothing. Get real support.

Remember there is truth to the saying "It is the journey not just the destination."

Guilt

"Guilt is an emotional state where we experience conflict at having done something that we believe we should not have done (or conversely, having not done something we believe we should have done)." ("Dealing with Feelings of Guilt - Cottesloe Counseling Centre")

This can give rise to a feeling or state which does not go away easily and can be difficult to manage. Sometimes guilt can feel so big that you may become overwhelmed and not know how to manage your feelings.

Guilt is an emotional warning sign that most people learn as a child. Its purpose is to let us know when we've done something wrong, and to help us develop a better sense of how we affect ourselves and others. It makes us re-examine things so that we don't make the same mistake twice.

As adults, it's amazing how quickly we feel guilty over the smallest things. Then guilt starts affecting you in ways you don't even realize. It starts to interfere with your decision-making. You may overwork or give too much of yourself. You may be willing to do anything in an attempt to make everyone happy. Or become overly critical about every action of yours and its possible consequences, even if this means that you are ignoring your needs and wants. You may become overly sensitive and sometimes it emotionally paralyzes you.

I met this amazing woman. She owns an online jewelry company that has been recognized as one of the top sellers in the country. She is positive, smart, and motivated. I was excited to meet with her to offer consulting services for her business.

And, the meeting went great. A week later, she sent me a note mentioning that she was not in a place to do that now, but she wanted to stay in touch. I was a little disappointed but not worried. I was happy to network with her and wanted to continue the good relationship. When she sent me the email, it was at a troubling time for me. My brother-in-law had just passed away from Covid and my sister was in a bad mental state. I was consumed with my personal life and never responded to her email.

Months later when things began to change, I regretted not responding to her email. Yet, it felt out of place to respond after all that time.

Six months later, I was working on the production of a backpack purse, and I needed a company to make charms for it. She would be the perfect person to make these for us, but I was hesitant to reach out to her because I still had my guilt for not responding to her email. I went back and forth in my brain for weeks before I got the guts to reach out to her. When I finally did, she was super excited to speak with me and met with me the very next day. I apologized for not responding to her email. To my surprise and relief, she remembered nothing of the incident and casually stated that the memory could have faded in her busy schedule.

My weeks of guilt and worry now lost all reason. Of course, I should have responded but I was letting guilt over something so small make business decisions for me. That was crazy!

We let guilt make all kinds of decisions for us and mostly we don't even realize. We let guilt talk us out of good advice or good decision-making. I have found that most times we do not realize that our guilt is affecting us in those ways, and it takes someone from the outside to see that.

One day at work, I was discussing with a friend the doubt I had about the information I had received from a production company.

LIFTING THE WEIGHT

My friend looked at me and said, "You need to ask the woman who used those factories and with whom you met."

Of course, that was the answer. As soon as she said it, I knew she was right. I knew that was the answer.

Why had I not thought of that?

Well, let's break that down... I had talked myself out of it before I even started. In my head, I had briefly thought of calling that woman for advice, but I had convinced myself that she did not have time for me, and that I would be an inconvenience to her. She may not have time to get back to me. It usually takes her a couple of days, but I had been sitting on this issue for 10 days already. My logic did not even make sense and it seems worse as I write it in this book.

My friend and I laughed about how simple things seem when you are outside a situation.

Some people tell you to look at your own situation from the outside but that is extremely hard to do. We are people and we have emotions and guilt over all kinds of different things that steer us.

Find the Right Fit

To be clear, I do not recommend you take advice from just anyone. When you need clarity and direction, I recommend you get advice from someone educated and trained to help you.

Every person or friend in your circle will give you advice based on their own biases about you and your situation. Sometimes that is okay but sometimes it is not a good fit. It is often better to have someone completely on the outside. It also allows you to speak more freely and not worry about being judged. This is especially helpful if you are going through something traumatic that others around you have a tough time understanding.

Often, we are not sure what the issue really is and need to talk about it to get to the root of things.

It might take more than one professional to find the right fit for you. Because we have our unique ways of establishing a connection with a person and sometimes it just doesn't click. Find a professional that you connect with and feel safe opening up to.

During one of my challenging times, I was talking to a counselor over the phone for a few weeks. I asked if I could talk to him twice a week instead of once a week. He said, "I am going to say no because I want to maintain some boundaries."

That really struck me the wrong way. I found a different professional to help me. I found a woman who was happy to talk with me two times a week for a couple of months as I got through the hardest phases and then we spoke less often. The first guy did not say anything wrong, and I was maybe a little too sensitive, but I got to choose whom I told my secrets to, and I wanted it to be someone I liked and connected with.

The first professional you talk to might not be the right fit. That is okay. Just find another one. I would say it is like having the right shoes. They have to be comfortable so you can walk in them. You do lots of walking in your shoes, and you cannot do that if they are not the right fit. Sometimes you think they are good at the store, and you take them home and they don't feel right. Or maybe after some use, they make your feet hurt. What do you do? You get a different pair. It is really that simple. You find a different professional that is a better fit.

I had a friend tell me she had six sessions with a girl and then quit. It took her several years to finally talk to someone again and the new counselor in one session accomplished more than the first counselor in six sessions.

Lifting the Weight

What does that look like coming out the other side? Well, I can tell you from experience that you feel stronger. You feel relief. You feel like you have more control over your life. You feel powerful, and to simplify things, you feel happy.

There is happiness that sneaks in.

Sometimes it does not even take very many sessions of counseling.

My husband and I were not getting along. I could not get him to talk to me. He said every time he tried it made me mad. That was true because he said things that hurt my feelings. I had no idea how we were going to work it out. One night we finally decided we needed outside perspective. His company had a counselor's contact. We sat on the bed and called in. We spoke to a counselor for maybe an hour. He helped us see things differently and from each other's perspective. We were able to take it from there. We worked it out and it only took one call.

That one call to ask for help relieved the pressure. The difference we felt in the days after was amazing. We learned an important piece about how we responded to each other. It gave us strength and the power to continue to fix things.

I am not saying everything in life will be better after one session but as you lift the weight it could be life-changing. You will have a clearer vision of how to move forward in your life. As the weights you carry start to come off, they will make room for the good and the positive. You will be able to make room in your brain to get things accomplished and do more of what you want to do in your life.

Pivotal Steps for Lifting the Weight

Step 1: Assess if you might need help moving your mental state forward. If you need help lifting the weight, get it. Get online or on the phone and get help. It is okay. It will make you stronger.

Step 2: Don't let guilt make your decisions.

Step 3: Find the right fit. It is worth trying until you find the right fit.

Step 4: Lift your weight and get motivated

Chapter Seven

You Are Unique

You are unique. Of all the people who have lived and died on earth not one of them has ever been exactly like
you.

You have something special to offer the world that no one else can.

You! You have different life experiences and perspectives that no one else can offer.

No one else has grown up exactly like you with the same brothers and sisters or lack of, the same animals, the same life moments. No one has the same talents and abilities or worked at the exact same jobs in the same positions and traveled to the same places, and loves the same way as you. No one has the same children or the same grandchildren. Once you start putting all those pieces together there is only one you.

I always thought, "You are special," is something only your mom tells you. Of course, not my mom because my mom who had me at 16 years old and my sister who was 11 months older than me at 15 did not tell me anything. She was busy partying and being mad at the world, so my sister and I got passed around the family and friends and sometimes in and out of foster homes. So, she never told me I was special but here I am over 40 and now I feel like I am special and have something great to offer.

I lived in Washington State. As I got older, I mostly lived with my 6 cousins whom I called my brothers and sister, my aunt, and my uncle whom I called my Daddy Boats. He went by Boats to everyone else because he was a Boats Mate in the Navy. With 7 kids there was no money. My Aunt did not really understand how to take care of kids and she did not know how to make food, so we were missing lots of basic necessities like food, socks, and bedsheets. My grandma was extremely sick, so she received cases of Osmolite nutrition formula free from the hospital. She would bring them over and that is what we lived off. Picture something similar to Ensure but since the formula was designed for feeding tubes it was not designed to taste good. We also had an apricot tree in the backyard and rhubarb that grew wild. My Aunt and Uncle were truly kind and compassionate, and you always knew they loved you.

I had my daughter at 19 who weighed only 1 pound and 4 ounces at birth. I went to work for a big-box retailer who continued raising me into a strong businesswoman. I married when I was 24 and the next year, we had a son. We moved across the country with my company. My husband has always been more domestic and maternal than I was, and we have always been great partners. I have lived through different traumas — friends getting addicted to opioids, friends losing their kids, close ones dying from cancer or living with cancer.

You might be able to relate to some of these things, but each of our stories is unique. You will have seen different things, lived and worked in different environments, and have different kids. Not only do we all have a different story with our kids, but they also grow up to be different people and our relationships with them give us all different learnings and failures.

Take time to think about your story.

- Where are you from?

- Who raised you?

- Do you have siblings or other kids you grew up with?

- What major decisions did you make in your teen years?

- What did you do as a young adult? Go to college, get married, have kids, drop out of college?

- What have been your major life experiences? You will have both good and bad.

Take time to write these things about you down. If you have a hard copy of this book, you will have a note page to write in.

What kind of learnings or successes do you have out of your life?

When I look back at my 18-year-old self, I remember telling my aunt that I was going off birth control. I said, "If I got pregnant, I guess that was supposed to happen." WOW! That was stupid!

Of course, my daughter was the best thing that ever happened to me. She made me get my act together. She makes me want to be more and do more in life so I could be better for her. Yet, we went through many hard years before that, which would have been nice to skip.

Think about your life and what you have been through. We discussed stupid things and hardships. What about some great things or some successes you have had? I continued to grow with the big-box retailer I worked for, from temporary seasonal help into one of the top-rated Store Managers in the nation.

I did not get there by not believing in myself. It was my job to believe in myself and have the determination to get me there.

It is your job to believe in yourself. That is right, I am telling you it is your job to believe in you!

You matter! You are special! You must know that in your heart.

Enjoy that uniqueness. It is something to be celebrated and special. You do not have to pretend to be someone else. You weren't meant to be like someone else. You were designed to be different. Nowhere, ever, in all of history will the same things be going in anyone's mind, soul, and spirit as the ones going on in yours right now. No one will be praying about the same things or dreaming about the same things. You are special. If you were not here on earth there would be a hole, a missing piece. No one can ever bring to the table exactly what you can.

All those things you wrote down earlier about yourself and your life journey are the things that make you unique. Now that you have written down all kinds of ways you are different from others, you can put that in your treasure box. You are your own treasure and a gift to the world. Enjoy being you and share yourself with others.

I share some of my stories with you and it must have sparked all different thoughts and emotions. No one else can reach others with their story in the same way you can. No one can speak from your experiences in the same words as you can. No one else will be able to bring the unique impact you have on another person.

No one has your smile. Or bring joy or cheer to a room like you. Share yourself with others. You matter and they are interested in your uniqueness.

Give yourself away! Let it inspire you and others! If you struggle to do that for yourself, you might need more help and that is okay.

There are things that you can do to help you. Find a ministry and learn about spiritual help or a counselor or a therapist.

You are unique and your learnings and life experiences have an influence on others. How you handle or mishandle your life experiences will give you and others key learnings. Sharing your stories and experiences can help others get through things. Sometimes hearing others' stories helps us all feel more normal and realize we are all imperfect.

You Can Do Anything!

We often tell our kids, "You can do anything you set your mind to." But is it truly accurate? Sometimes, even the act of verbalizing this idea may be met with doubt and uncertainty. Can you really do anything? Sometimes when I want something and I don't go after it, I realize I have convinced myself that I am not good enough or I don't deserve it.

Well, I am here to tell you that there is truth to what we tell our kids. You can do anything you set your mind to. It might not be easy, and you will need help and support.

- You will need people who are experts in different areas around you.

- You will have to start moving before the entire path is laid out.

- Even if you had the whole thing laid out it may change.

- Things will change every day, every step of the way. Even though things will change along the way, you will get it if you continue working towards it.

- It is okay if you change your mind. Let me repeat. It is okay if you change your mind along the way.

- Changing your mind in the middle of the process does not make you a failure! Even if you failed at the goal, you have learned and achieved so much.

Now, here is the caveat; you might think you want something, set your mind to it, and as you're moving towards it, realize that you no longer want it or that what you've gained along the way is not worth giving up. It's important to question your motivations and desires occasionally.

Here are some ideas.

- Acknowledge your accomplishments: When we get something done it makes us feel good no matter how small. Look through your Good Job folder or your Thankful journal.

- Words of affirmation: Spoken or written words that confirm, support, and uplift you. You could put sticky notes on your desk or your bathroom mirror that say good things about you. Repeat them over and over again.

- Get some support: A counselor, therapist, or a support group.

- Share what you have to offer: Share your unique skills and abilities with someone else. Helping others strengthens our belief in ourselves.

Let's just say for a minute that this chapter helped with your belief in yourself and you are ready to move forward.

Ask yourself, "What do I want?"

Make a list of the things you want in your life. What is meaningful to you?

Knowing who you are and your unique qualities is enormously powerful. It matters in your life, and it will help you live your best life and help make a difference in others' lives.

Pivotal Steps to Believing You Are Unique

Step 1: Write down the facts about yourself. Get into the weeds. List major life experiences, things you learned, things you messed up, and things you did well.

Step 2: You matter. Share your story. Others want to hear it.

Step 3: Believe in yourself and set your mind to what you want.

Step 4: Make a list of the things you want in your life.

Chapter Eight

The Green Monster

LET'S TALK ABOUT JEALOUSY. Nobody likes to be called jealous. If you told me I was jealous, that would probably piss me off. Yet, we do all kinds of things we don't even realize out of jealousy or spite. That is why I call it the green monster. It takes over like a monster from within you. We are just going to take this from 'her' perspective but for you men that might have been brave enough to read this book. You do it too. The definition of jealousy is feeling or showing envy of someone or their achievements and advantages. Or I would say perceived advantages.

THE GREEN MONSTER

Suppose a beautiful, young woman walks up and does the same things as you in your job. It is like an uncontrollable instinct kicked in to dislike her. Let's just start by admitting that it is jealousy. We almost can't help it. It's not like we're trying to be jealous or mean or not like other people. It just happens and once it does, we have too much pride to take it back.

Let's explore this scenario. Why is it that we don't want to like her? Obviously, it's not about her at all. It's about you. It's about your own insecurities. It's about how you feel like you don't stack up. Or about how you feel you are not good enough. Your hair is not as long. Your shoes are not as cute. You're not as pretty. You're not as nice. You feel your friends and coworkers will like her better than you.

So, the reality is it's about you. It's not about her at all. At first, we don't even realize our intentions when we do some of the horrible things to other people out of jealousy.

What about your friend who comes to you super excited about a new idea? They want to go change the world and do something big and major and you're like, "What are you thinking?"

"Have you lost your mind?"

"Are you sure you can do that?"

"Why would you do that?"

"Why do you even want to do that?"

All these naysayer things that we say to them are because we're afraid for them or because of all these excuses we give ourselves. The reality is we're just jealous that they have the balls to go and try to do that and we didn't.

I have been jealous so many times in my life and career. I think of the time when I was pregnant, and a co-worker of my husband was hanging out with him a lot. She went to lunch with him and shared all kinds of personal things with him. The problem was not her or him, it was me. He was not doing anything wrong, but I was mad and jealous

THE GREEN MONSTER

that I was pregnant and stuck on bed rest, and I could not go to lunch or even go to work. You see I was on my second baby. My first child, my daughter who was born at Week 24 and weighed only 1 lb. 4 oz at the time of birth, was the youngest baby born in Washington State that lived. She was in the neonatal intensive care unit for four and a half months. So, the doctors had to put me on bed rest since Week 24 for my second pregnancy. I could not go anywhere or do anything, I could only lay there and watch TV, cry, and scream. My jealousy was about me and what I could or couldn't do, not what he or she was or wasn't doing. My husband is an incredibly loyal and great man and we have been married for 20 years now.

When you come to the understanding that individuals you don't like are more a reflection of yourself than they are of themselves, it opens the door to start actively working on liking others more. Taking the time to learn more about them and developing more compassion and understanding towards them improves your ability to be a better support system for them and makes you a better person overall. We tell all kinds of stuff to ourselves in our heads that is not true.

"My hair is too short or too thin or too brown."

"My nose is too small or too big or my eyes are not shaped right."

"My lips are too small or too big."

"I am too fat or too skinny or my butt is not shaped right."

"I am not smart enough or educated enough."

"I don't come from a good enough family."

All these self-sabotaging sentences in our head! We talked about self-talk already and the things it can stop you from doing.

When we come across someone who makes us feel jealous or does something better than us, we often let it make us feel bad about ourselves. In response, we lash out and try to make them feel less so we feel better. I am not sure why this even makes us feel better. Maybe it is our competitive spirit. Everyone likes to win.

Unfortunately, the worst part is when we start to react to these emotions by excluding that person, ignoring them, or giving them dirty looks. We shut down their ideas and make them feel stupid, in an attempt to make them as insecure as we feel.

Sometimes we even say only mean things to them under the disguise of helping them.

Supporting Through Jealousy

I had a good friend whom I helped find inspiration and motivation. I sparked great ideas in her and encouraged her to do more in her life. She was interviewed for a CEO position. I had previously told her I wanted to work for a non-profit. A couple of months later, I showed up at her house to bring her lunch and she was getting the call that she has just been selected as the new CEO of a local nonprofit. I was so happy for her, but it was hard to swallow. I had not even been interviewed. Of course, I had not even started applying either. I was able to recognize instantly as my stomach tightened and I felt like vomiting and a cold, nasty feeling came over me. I was able to recognize my jealousy right away and then put a big smile on my face and gave her the biggest hug.

Remember that others cannot hear what you are thinking. What matters is that you SAY and DO the right thing.

Here was this amazing Latinx woman who deserved all the greatness life has to offer and she is an amazing leader. I have found myself proud to follow her several times in my career. Her advice is always solid and meaningful. Other than me having occasional spurts of jealousy looking at her, the owner of the company she was working for was also jealous. Instead of showing support for this amazing woman at a time when a leader like her is really needed in our community, he just said all kinds of un-supporting things. He put down the new company she was going to work for and told her how much better she would be if she stayed at his company.

I was so sad for her when she told me about that. But I knew why he said all those things. It was about him and not her. Most people are going to react like him. And then once we react like that, we're going to tell ourselves that is because we are looking out for our friends and colleagues. We are trying to protect them and do what we think is best for them. That is B.S. If that is what you do, knock it off. You are not helping or supporting.

Switch to the other side. Be one of the people supporting others and not tearing them down.

How to Recognize You Are Jealous and Use It to Your Benefit?

Jealousy is often a sign of insecurity. Or it could mean you have identified something you want. I realized that I was jealous of my friend when she got promoted to CEO. At that moment, I knew that I wanted to be a CEO of a company. Prior to that, I had not been certain of what I wanted to do in my career. One can choose to address this realization by identifying something in their life they want to change or pursue. For me, the realization that I wanted to be a CEO prompted me to start my own company. Now, I am the CEO of my own company. Sometimes, we do not realize what we want until we see others achieving it.

- The trick is acknowledging that you are getting jealous.

- Figure out what you are jealous of.

- Decide if that's what you really want.

- Figure out how to use that to your

advantage and go get it.

If someone else has something that you want, you could simply ask them how they got it, and follow their path or pave your own.

I was at a networking meeting. I saw a woman who had changed her hair and it was stunning. To be specific, she had extensions put in her hair. She looked beautiful. Her hair was amazing. I really thought it was the most beautiful hair I had ever seen. As I was complimenting her on her hair, I got that pang in my stomach. I instantly felt like I did not like her. I realized right away I was jealous. Okay so, if her hair makes me that jealous what was I going to do about it? Do I want to get extensions? I asked her about it and made a plan and I will let you know how it turns out. I had to decide if I was willing to do the work to take care of it and pay the money.

Recognize and Remove

There is another thing about jealousy. There will be times when you cannot help someone else not be jealous of you. You will come across times in your life when you will need to recognize the jealousy someone else has for you and remove yourself from the environment because the other person may not be able to control their emotions. When it comes to that, consider it a compliment that you are that good and that strong.

As you continue to gain confidence, you will run into this more. Some people will never change their behavior and will continue to be toxic to you, regardless of their role in your life - whether it's a boss, sister, best friend, brother, parent, co-worker, or significant other.

My sister and I were living together. We were going to work on losing weight. It was January and she made a big deal about how she was not going to help anyone else. She made plans to order specially prepared meals from a food packaging company, had a book of weight loss recipes, got a digital online trainer, and repeatedly emphasized that she wasn't going to help anyone else — meaning me.

She wasn't going to "Wipe anyone's ass." I was totally good with that, and I had my own agenda anyway.

I was not worried about what she was doing, and I was confident in my plans. I was doing shakes and a T-25 exercise routine daily. I was losing weight regularly and stayed happy with my own plan.

She could not stand it! She was mad that I had a different food plan that was working. She was always trying to push her food on me. It made her crazy that I was not after her plan. She was nasty and aggressive about every decision I made. My shakes were "stupid". She was angry that I worked out early in the mornings instead of late at night when she liked to work out. She got nasty and aggressive about everything.

It took me a while to realize that it was because she was jealous. She was worried that if I lost more weight than her, then her journey was not good enough. The longer we lived together the more she acted like that in every aspect of our lives. Her insecurity rose with my confidence. I love her very much, but this was no way to live.

She should not always have to feel insecure, and I did not deserve to be treated horribly every day due to her insecurities. That year we decided we probably should not live together anymore. I knew she loved and cared about me, but she could not help herself. She needed to tear me down to make herself feel better. She could not get herself to be nice and supportive of me even when we were close. That was no way for either of us to live. These days we love each other from a distance.

Recognizing individuals in your life who consistently tear you down and are unable to be supportive is a significant step. To protect yourself, it may be necessary to distance yourself from them. Keep in mind, you cannot control the actions of others; you can only make decisions for yourself.

Pivotal Steps to Dealing With Your Green Monster

Step 1: Start recognizing when you are jealous of someone else. You know by now I am going to tell you to write it down.

Step 2: Write down what insecurities that jealousy is playing to. Write down what your jealousy is telling you about yourself. Make a list of what you plan to do about it.

Step 3: Support others around you through your jealousy. Remember others cannot hear or feel your thoughts and you always have the opportunity to do and say the right thing.

Step 4: Use your jealousy to your benefit. Use it to motivate you into action and achieve your dreams.

Step 5: Recognize it in others and remove yourself if needed.

Chapter Nine

Ask for What You Want

At work, I was asked to join a new project. It started with a piece of white paper with the words "Pathway program" scribbled in the middle with a cloud and lines coming out of it that had words like "two years and learning, leadership, rewards, videos, mobile devices, associates at all levels," etc.

I took that piece of paper, we added more ideas, and we started fleshing it out. We got other subject matter experts involved and

ASK FOR WHAT YOU WANT 127

within two years we turned that piece of paper into a billion-dollar training pathway for 2.5 million associates across the US.

My point is you need to start somewhere.

I say, start by writing it down.

Write down what you want to do. Where do you want to go? Do you want a new house, a new car, a better job, or a different boss? Do you want to go on more vacations, and do more things with your family?

Get it on paper or make a list on your phone.

Once you start getting it out of your head and onto paper it starts to become real. It gets better and more focused over time. It does not start out as something great. You make it great as you think more about it and get input from others. You continue to focus on it, add to it, and make it better. You will talk about it with others, and they will contribute great ideas.

I was writing this book and explaining a few chapters, and someone said to me, "You should add blank note pages so people can write in it like a workbook."

Loved the idea. If you have a physical copy, you will have those pages to see how far you have really come.

Get started. Your mind has the power to make amazing things happen. It is your job to get the ball rolling. If you need help, there are people who can help you get to where you want to go. As for those who don't believe in you or try to pull you back, we'll save that for another chapter.

Coach

Get yourself a coach who specializes in the area you are wanting to go. So, if it is to grow your business, get a business coach. If it is being better at financials, get a financial coach. If it is moving your life forward, get a life coach. Another great place to get coaching is from a professional in the field you are interested in. They can share with you their journey and you can make decisions for yourself based on their path.

ASK FOR WHAT YOU WANT

I have found that most people at any level in business will meet with you to talk about themselves. It is a human's favorite thing to do. It is a Win-Win; they get to talk about themselves which boosts their confidence and you get to learn valuable things to use in your life.

I have had the opportunity to meet with several high-level executives and Fortune 500 CEOs just by asking if they would mind sharing their stories with me. I have learned mountains of things from those conversations. I have learned how to get different things done in my life as well. I learned small things like how they decide to dress and big things that really made a difference.

I asked an Executive Vice President if she would meet with me, and I was incredibly disappointed with the conversation. She did not seem that interested in talking to me even though she took the meeting. The only thing she really said was, "Even if you don't care for the job you are doing, dig in and learn as much as you can about that role. The more you dig in and learn in every position the better off you will be."

At the time, her words failed to make sense to me. 'Learn what you are doing'? Duh! Isn't that what everyone does? As weeks passed, I couldn't get her words out of my head. After all, she is an EVP and if she believed that was the most valuable advice she could give me, I should listen. I put it to work and dug into what I was doing. I learned about the company finances, profit and loss, automating data entry to PowerPoint presentations, and over time ended up taking the role of our finance person when she left.

The skills also came in handy years later when I left the big corporate world and started my own small business. Having a strong financial acumen is why I was able to open, grow, and sell my small business in 4 years.

Sometimes you don't even realize what you learn from a conversation. It can work in smaller ways as well. Say you want a new car, and you don't know where to start. Ask someone you know who has a nice car how they got it. Maybe ask a few people. Then they might say, "I got a loan from a bank." Great! Go talk to a bank about how car loans work. They might say, "I bought it from a car lot." Go to a car lot.

There are always people that can help you figure things out. But you must start looking for those people in the first place. Pick a direction. Your mind is a powerful tool. Use it to your benefit.

Vision Boards Are a Great Tool

Let me give you an example. I was working for a retail company in the stores. I did an excellent job, and I was always called in to save the day, fix the store, or make big things happen in a very short amount of time. I had been called to empty forty trailers in five days, stock ten semi-trucks of freight, and clean up an entire store in three days, to save people's jobs. I was always willing and had lots of success and awards, but my ultimate want was to become the Store Manager. No matter what I accomplished they always picked the other guy.

So, I decided — let me say that again since it is an important phrase in moving your life forward — *I decided* I was going to figure out how to be a Store Manager.

I took the recap paper that came out every day and highlighted the title Store Manager and hung it in my file cabinet drawer. I highlighted a new one every week. Every time I opened my file cabinet and saw that, it prompted me to get to the next step.

I spoke to my Store Manager and my Market Manager. I was told lots of things that I did not want to hear. I was told that I had to value others' opinions more and recognize different perspectives. Those were true, yet I did not like them. I read Dale Carnegie's book *How to Win Friends*

ASK FOR WHAT YOU WANT 133

and Influence People, again. I studied the chapters ("Dale Carnegie's communication tips — Transformative Conversations") and put them into practice, again.

Apparently, despite the mental and emotional growth I achieved, I always looked the same in the eyes of the people around me. If I really wanted a chance, then I must move away from the people I had grown up with. I needed somewhere fresh to put my new-found knowledge and expertise to practice. I decided to move my family halfway across the country to start new and continue to grow into the kind of Store Manager I could be. I had to make some tough decisions, get out of my comfort zone, and do some scary stuff if I wanted to reach my goal. I moved my family from Spokane, Washington to Tulsa, Oklahoma and went on to become a great store manager. I became the best store manager I could have ever dreamed of, and I was rated as the top store manager in my category and offered a position to come to the corporate office and help open 500 more stores just like mine across the country. That all started with me deciding to act on what I wanted.

The Universe Cannot Help You if You Don't Ask

That's right! You have to ask for what you want.

I was always taught to keep my head down and work hard and expect recognition to come my way. You might have had a similar training, too.

Well, it turns out that this idea becomes true only when your boss is a great leader and has the power to recognize or promote you. That is an uncommon combination these days. You have to ask for what you want. You have to ask the universe. You have to ask your life partner. You have to ask your friends, your kids, and your boss. You have to ask for lots of reasons. Not just because they will give it to you if you ask, but because you need to understand more about how

ASK FOR WHAT YOU WANT

to get what you want. Start by asking the universe.

What does that mean? Start by writing it down. Say it out loud. Pray for it. If you are not putting it out there, it cannot come to you. Why do you think vision boards work so well? Why do you think athletes have visualization exercises?

When you start asking, it comes to the top of your mind often.

- You start noticing things that relate to what you want.

- You learn so many things about what you want.

- You learn what other things you might have to do to get it.

- You will realize who is and is not supporting you.

- You start meeting people who have done what you want to do and others that can help you get there.

If you want to do something in your company and your company won't let you, there are a million other companies out there.

When I was younger, I was afraid to ask for what I wanted. I was afraid to say it out loud. I was embarrassed to think I wanted more. I feared rejection from my boss and coworkers. So, I just kept working hard and hoped someone would make it their idea. Some did but some did not. I was so scared of their thoughts and opinions. When I was in my early 20's I wanted to be a Co-Store manager and I kept getting overlooked. So, I finally spoke to my Market Manager. By the time I had the guts to speak to him, I had let all the anguish and feelings overwhelm me for months. I was terrified of the conversation. I could barely talk without wanting to cry. What he told me was not what I wanted to hear but it was true, and I took his advice. If I had never had that conversation, I would have never understood what it would take to get to the next level.

There Is Enough to Go Around

No matter what idea you have there is enough to go around. In 2017, Sabrina opened a painting company in her town. There were already several other painting companies. She had plenty of competition. However, she did not worry about that. She just focused on giving her customers the best experience possible and she was able to do about $30,000 in sales a month. Had she worried about the competition instead of focusing on being the best she could be, she would not have been successful and been able to sell her remarkably successful painting company 4 years later.

Sometimes, we become overly concerned about what others are doing, or if they may replicate our ideas unethically. This can cause us to hold back from moving forward, and we may not share our goals with others out of fear. However, it's important to remember that most people are supportive and want to help us succeed. So, let me just do some myth-busting for you. Even if someone else tries to do something similar, they will bring their own experiences and background to the task, resulting in a different outcome. No one will ever do it exactly like you. There are always many brands and knock-offs for every type of product. Yet, there is a customer for everyone. There is a market for a $1,000 purse, as well as a $100 purse; a $100 pair of shoes, a $200 pair of shoes, and a $1000 pair of shoes.

Once you turn your needs and ideas into reality, you effectively breathe life into your idea. You are starting to make it happen. You must believe that there is abundance in the world, and you are deserving of that abundance.

Heather and her boyfriend Billy live together in a small studio apartment. They each had minimum-wage jobs and they really wanted a truck. They did not have a lot of money or good credit, but they really wanted a truck. Billy told his boss and his coworkers he was looking for a truck. He talked about it to his family, and they looked at trucks all the time. One day Billy's boss said he met a guy who might have a truck that was a good fit, but it was in another town. Billy ended up working a deal to get the truck. Now, if Billy had not told anyone what he wanted he would never have gotten the truck. Also, it was easy for Billy and Heather to believe there are plenty of different trucks in the world. Sometimes it is not as easy for us to believe that there is an abundance of what we need or want, especially if our exposure has been limited. Don't worry about others, focus on yourself. Think about what you want. Tell yourself there is plenty of that in the world. I am writing this book to support others in reaching their goals and dreams and I have to believe that there are lots of people in the world that will read it and that it will add value to their lives.

Learn or Find Someone Who Already Knows

You are not going to know everything so stop trying!

You don't have to know exactly how to get what you want.

You don't have to know all the steps or even any of them.

There is always someone who knows the stuff you don't. You don't have to figure everything out yourself. It is okay to ask for help and more importantly to accept help. If there is something you cannot do or don't know how, find someone who does. There are also going to be things you don't want to learn or struggle learning. Find someone who already knows it and use their knowledge. Most people are willing to share their knowledge. It makes people feel good to help you. It makes people feel valuable. Now, that is not to say don't do anything on your own but don't let what you don't know stop you.

Pivotal Steps To Ask for What You Want

Step 1: Write down what you want. Make a list or a paragraph. I use a dream box. Tear it up into little scraps of paper and put them in the box. However, you do it, get it out of your head.

Step 2: Tell others what you want. Tell them your goals and your dreams. Let people tell you "NO". Every "NO" teaches you something and gets you closer to yes!

Step 3: Make a visualization with an abundance mindset. Make a vision board or highlight the words to look at every day. Do visualization exercises. Visualize what you want.

Step 4: Build on others' knowledge. If people aren't offering it willingly then seek it.

Chapter Ten

Financial Security Matters

When you feel like you have a solid financial footing you make better decisions. You take bigger steps because you feel like you have a cushion if it does not work. You are not as desperate. You don't keep a job where you are treated poorly. You go after what you want with more confidence.

What Does Financial Security Mean?

This question can be hard to answer because most of us have been told in our childhoods that it is rude or inappropriate to talk about money. It depends on how old you are. If you are young and you have $500 in savings, then you feel financially secure. Once you start paying all your own bills, then $1500 in your savings would make you feel secure. Financial security means different things to different people. Yes, there are some guidelines, but you need to answer the question — What does financial security mean to me?

To me, it means being on track to retire at 65 and thereafter live on the money saved. Until 90, perhaps. I have a steady income. I have the money to pay my bills each month and a little extra for fun. I have money for two vacations a year and I have money in savings. For more details on this read my next book Save, Pivotal Solutions for Your Finances.

Financial security is a state of mind. My husband and I were in our early thirties, and we had maxed out all our credit cards. We spent them on all kinds of things like, eating out, Christmas presents for kids, and a vacation to Disney World.

The day-to-day struggle of paying these credit card bills as they continued to pile up got increasingly stressful. Some months we were barely able to afford the credit card bills and our regular bills.

Of course, this caused us to continue relying on our credit cards. We would repeat the cycle every month: make credit card payments and then use the newfound room on our credit cards to pay for that month's bills. It was an endless cycle of overwhelm and caused constant fear of bankruptcy. The credit card debt had become so unmanageable that it led to arguments and fights. I was unsure of how to proceed and handle the situation.

My husband and I were taught the importance of saving for retirement from a young age. However, at a certain point, we began to question if it would be wiser to use our retirement savings to pay off debt. I am glad to say we did not make that decision. Our financial advisor, who is a wise person, advised us differently when we consulted him. He asked us several questions.

"Are you paying all of your bills?"

"Well, yes, of course."

"Are you behind on anything?"

"No, of course, not."

"So, all your bills are paid and up to date?"

"Yes, they're all up to date"

"Let me explain something to you. Your problem is a state of mind."

At first, it pissed me off. A state of freaking mind? It's not going to be a state of mind when I go bankrupt!

He continued, "Your problem isn't where you're at financially, your problem is how you feel about where you're at financially."

He went on to explain that there are millions of people all over the world who had failed to pay rent and credit card bills for 6-8 months and that they've gone to collection.

"You're not in any of that kind of shape. You're just very worried."

Well, I guess that was true.

FINANCIAL SECURITY MATTERS 147

Then he said, "Okay, let's do this, you are already paying all your bills, but you have no money left over." He suggested we look at our bank statements together. We reviewed 3 months' worth of bank statements. We found a lot of coffee and eating out and then he talked to us about what we could do about those. We can make coffee at home. We can start making dinner at home.

The craziest thing about this entire conversation is how I felt afterward.

Before we had the conversation, I felt overwhelmed and believed that something terrible would happen due to the debt we had accumulated. Negative self-talk consumed me, and I felt embarrassed and guilty. But after the conversation, I felt relieved and motivated. We had a plan, and I knew we could make small changes, such as making coffee at home and planning out dinners, to save money and spend less. Our goal was to pay off one credit card at a time and make a plan for them. To get more details, read my next book Save, Pivotal Solutions for Your Finances.

I had a plan. I had focus. I was motivated. Suddenly, I could handle all of it. My husband and I did go on to pay off all our credit cards and became debt-free. We did get ourselves back into lots of debt several more times over the next 20 years, but we always managed to get out, too.

Financial Visibility Matters

If your finances are in good shape and you don't have any financial woes, please skip this chapter and move on. If you could use a few tips and tad bits that have a proven track record, then read my next book Save, Pivotal Solutions for Your Future.

To get control of your finances you must have the full picture of your finances. Know how much money is coming in and how much is going out. Collect your bills and make a list. Make a list on your phone or make a spreadsheet. You need full visibility. You need a list of every one of your bills and their due date. If it is a credit card, include your interest rate. Cross-verify your bills with your bank statements and catch auto withdrawals, as well.

Once you figure out how much you have coming in, review your bank statements with this number in mind. I am sure you will see things you can do differently. Cancel the gym memberships or other subscriptions that you don't use well.

Getting full visibility of your financial picture is the first step to financial well-being. You cannot and will not be able to understand your financial situation if you cannot see it. Get it on paper.

Maybe you have even tried making a budget. I would tell you a budget is the most useful for planning for the future, like helping young people understand how much they will need to make at their jobs. Making a budget as an adult mostly ends with a lack of money to do all the things you want to do and quickly out the window goes the budget.

If you are a great budgeteer and it has worked for you, then excellent. Keep up the excellent work and you probably should have skipped this chapter already.

I recommend a strategy that goes like this.

- Pay your bills.

- Buy food and your necessities.

- Pay yourself in your savings or retirement or both.

- Play.

Let me tell you how it went for Tabitha. She was 24 and she had gotten herself in a financial mess. She was over-drafting her bank account daily and was at her overdraft limit of $500. Her part of the rent with her roommate was a month behind. Her portion was $400, and she had just lost her job and found a new one, but she wasn't going to get paid for another 2 weeks. Her car payment and her insurance were overdue. In all, she was about $1500 in the hole. The worst part was feeling like she was drowning. She was ashamed and afraid to tell anyone about her situation. She had no money for food or gas. How did we start to get her back on track with her financial future?

Shelter, Ability to get to work, Debt, and Necessities. Of course, we had to change her mindset and make a plan.

FINANCIAL SECURITY MATTERS 151

She had to first stop the bleeding. Stop using her debit card while in overdraft. The charges amounted to $25 each time. To do that, we took her debit card and put it in a Ziplock bag full of water, and stuck it in the freezer. Freezing it literally. Now if she wanted to use it, she would have to wait for it to defrost, giving her time to think about her decision.

Then she borrowed money to pay her rent to keep her shelter. She had three babysitting and dog-watching jobs that week. That money was transferred to her electronically so it would be directly deposited into her account.

We made a 3-prong approach.

1. All money from her day job goes to pay for her car, insurance, and the loan for her rent payment.

2. All money from babysitting and dog watching goes to get her bank account out of the negative.

3. She reached out to everyone she knew, asking if they had any jobs that they were willing to pay her to do. She used this cash for food and gas. She

got a few jobs cleaning windows, baseboards, and a few other things.

4. Then she planned to move forward. She got her bills on an app on her phone, sorted them by due date, and separated what she will pay with her first payday of the month and what she will pay on her second payday. She canceled all her subscriptions and stopped anything that was automatically withdrawn until she had more control.

Within 45 days Tabitha had dug herself out of the hole and was back on track. She also found a better living situation that cost a little more and she had the money to move.

Pay yourself first! You matter!

Why pay yourself? When you have money in savings it gives you the feeling of financial security. It gives you a sense of deep pride and confidence which in turn give you more strength and better judgment when making life decisions.

For instance, an emergency savings account can save you from working for someone who treats

FINANCIAL SECURITY MATTERS 153

you poorly. Because you have the money to pay your rent for a month or two while you find a new job. It gives you room to breathe if you lose your job unexpectedly or have a medical or dental bill.

What does paying yourself look like? It looks like building accounts that take care of you. Emergency savings and retirement accounts.

The most important part is not the number but the will to get started. Save for your retirement every month. That is one way to get started. Start with 1% of each paycheck. Then add 1% every couple of months until you get to 6% to 10% or until it hurts and then maybe pull back a little.

It could be as little as $5 a month or $20 a month. If you're serious, it could be $100 a month or $200 a month. The amount is not as important as the consistency of doing it.

Even if you're living from paycheck to paycheck, as much as $200 in your savings account could give you the confidence you need to make the right decisions to move forward in your life.

The crazy thing about retirement accounts is if you start them when you are 20 you will probably be a millionaire with a much smaller investment. However, most of us don't start working on them until we are in our 40s. For more details on achieving financial security, read my next book Save, Pivotal Solutions for Your Finances.

Pivotal Steps to Moving Toward Financial Security

Step 1: Acknowledge and gain clarity on your current state of mind regarding your financial security.

Step 2: Gain visibility of your full financial situation. Understand your income and expenses by putting them on paper.

Step 3: Pay yourself, always! Start today!

Chapter Eleven

Dig Out the GRIT!

WHAT IS GRIT?

My son came to me one day and asked, "Mom, do I have grit?" He was so worried about failing in college. His professor had told him that, to be successful in college he has to have grit. He assumed he had none and was set to fail. I could tell by his tone; he was afraid of my answer. I looked him straight in the eyes and said, "Yes of course you have grit. You are my son!"

I saw his eyes get big and wide with excitement and relief. He was 16 years old and in 11th grade, already taking full college load at the community college along with his Highschool PE & Economics class. The

DIG OUT THE GRIT! 157

kid is amazing, and yet he had to come and ask me if he had grit. These are the kinds of things we all do to ourselves

When I was young, my life goals were to make it past 15 before I had a baby and graduate high school, since I would be the first one in three generations to do so. As I graduated high school, I found myself 19 years old with a baby girl born weighing 1 pound 4 ounces at only 24 weeks since gestation. Her dad had a drinking problem and I decided to get an apartment together but neither of us had a job or any money. We found someone who let us use the upstairs of his bar area as an apartment. My Aunt came and helped me frame a wall between the bathroom and the kitchen. It was not great, but this place was close to the hospital. We could see our daughter in the Neonatal Intensive Care Unit every 4 hrs. For 15 minutes per visit. This went on for 4 months. As she grew and lived past all expectations, at about 4 months they said she would be able to come home in 3 weeks.

What?? I could not bring her home. What home? My Aunt was in Germany for the military and my uncle smoked in the house. My baby had already had a collapsed lung and could not be around cigarette smoke. She was only 4 lbs.

I could not imagine bringing my little baby to this nasty place above a bar. I had no idea how to do it or where to start but I knew I had to find a better place to live, and I only had 3 weeks to do so. I had a little book someone had given me with community support numbers and places in it. I sat down and started calling each number explaining my situation and asking if they could help me or if they knew someone who could. When they said no, I just called the next number.

After several days of making calls and getting referred to other people, I found someone who recommended a home healthcare nurse. She knew of an apartment complex that took low-income or homeless families. Since our apartment was not legally considered an apartment, we were already legally homeless.

I spoke with the apartment every day to see if they had any openings. A few days before my baby was supposed to come home, we were able to move into our new apartment. I was determined not to let my 4lb baby come home with no place to live after fighting for her life for 4 months. I did not know anything, and I certainly had no answers, but I just kept asking until someone could help me.

I was determined. It took everything inside of me to keep calling numbers and pouring my heart out just for them to tell me they could not help. I could not afford to have too much pride or to give up. I had to dig inside of myself and **find that grit!** I had to tighten that rock in my stomach and keep going. We all have that inside of us.

We don't have to be in a dire situation to use it. We can dig it out any time we need it. It is a mindset. It is a lot easier to find when you are mad or fed up or desperate. Everyone has a different level of desperation. Your level of desperation is based on your life experiences.

You don't have to be desperate to call on that grit inside of you, however, if you think back to a time when you were desperate it might be easier to recall that feeling that made you fight for what you wanted or needed.

You have value and you have strength. There is no one in this world that gets through this life unscathed. No one gets off with no heartbreak. You have been through tough times. You have survived. You have it in you to keep pushing forward. You have grit somewhere. Some of us have a harder time finding our grit than others. Sometimes, you have to channel anger or other strong emotions. We all have it. Some of us have a little too much of it. I might fit in that category.

When I worked in the stores as an hourly supervisor, I remember my Market Manager used to call it "fire in your belly."

He told a coworker of mine, Marcus, that he would not promote him because he did not have enough fire in his belly. He thought Markus was too laid back and did not have enough grit. That really pissed Marcus off and he stormed out. I guess he found his fire. Marcus ended up getting promoted.

Think through your life. Think about the times when you had to use your own grit to get through something. Picture how you felt. Were you angry, mad, or determined? Did your stomach tighten? Did it feel like your body was stiffer? I recommend you take some time and write it down. You already wrote about your life in another chapter. These times were life-changing events. It could be a little less dramatic event as well.

When my daughter was in first grade, I would go to help at her school. She was a quiet sweet little girl. She did not draw much attention. I was worried that she was not learning. She is my first child, and I did not know what was wrong. I expressed my concerns to her teacher who was also the part-time Principal. This was a very low-income school system so the turnover in teachers was high and the kids that got the attention were the troublemakers because there were so many of them. She said my daughter was doing fine. By the time we got to second grade, I was sure there was an issue, and it took several months to get the school to listen. I had to contact the Superintendent. I fought with her school all through her second grade because they insisted she was fine. She had no work or writing in her notebooks. She could not spell. I took her to an outside party to have her tested and they told us she was at least a year behind. I petitioned the district to let me move her to an out-of-district school. Finally, in the third grade in the new school, they tested her and found she had a learning disability.

This part of my life was not as extreme as some of the things in prior years. I still needed to dig out my grit to get to the bottom of it. Now that you know what grit is. You should be able to see where you have used it in your own life. This next part will go a lot easier if you have 2 or 3 specific stories in your life to think about as you go. It is easy for us to move forward in life and forget the hard work we did to get there.

How to Use Your Grit?

Let's talk about how you can recall your grit and how to use it. You are going to start by using your past stories of when you used grit to motivate you forward. Think about the feeling you had when you were determined to get through.

When I use my grit, it looks something like this.

I block my mind like a brick wall. I make an effort to stop all the self-talk and second-guessing. I clear everything except what I am going to do. I push all my other worries and concerns to the side. I can physically feel my body stiffen and clench like I am getting ready for a fight. My voice gets more solid and in charge. I walk with power and motivation, and I do whatever it is I need to do and don't think about anything else until my next move is made.

It might look and feel differently for you and that is totally okay.

You don't have to be going through tough times to put your grit to use in your everyday life. It is a valuable tool that can help you push through fear and failure and even just keep you on track as you take on new scary paths in your life. Use that grit to keep you going as things get hard and you get unsure of yourself. Recall the things you have been through and use them to support you as you walk through your life which is in front of you now.

The interesting thing about grit is that we find it so easy to call upon it to defend someone. If someone else needs help or needs us, no matter what is going on, we make time and room for them. We find the strength to defend or support them. I have a friend who calls it the Mama Bear in me. Some term it the maternal or paternal instinct. It just comes right out for other people. It is so much harder for us to do it for ourselves.

Let's do for ourselves what we are willing to do for others. Tell yourself, "I am going to use my Grit to help and support me!" Starting today it is time to use it for you, too.

Pivotal Steps to Dig Out Your Grit and Use It

Step 1: Write 3-5 stories of when you used grit for yourself or someone else.

Step 2: Recall those feelings. Mentally and physically. How did your body react? What was your mindset? Write those things down.

Step 3: Identify what is going on in your life today that you could use grit for. Make a list. Pick one and start using that Grit for you.

Chapter Twelve

Build a Support System

Coaches and Cheerleaders

It may sound like you are building a sports team. Let's just go with the sports analogy for a minute. Take a football team. They have coaches with different expertise that dig into different areas of the team. You need the same situation for different areas of your life. They have cheerleaders who keep the energy and excitement in between the big plays.

I have a friend who is a great cheerleader. Her name is Angela, she is always excited about what I am doing, and she always makes me feel like a superwoman. I love being around her and when we part, I am always motivated to move forward. In some way, she gives me strength. We all need a friend like her.

It takes the entire team to do their part for the star player to make the touchdown. You are always the star player of your life. Having support in all these different areas is what helps you reach your goals.

Mentors

Someone asked me what I thought of mentors. Well, that is a loaded question. I have had plenty of mentors that helped me through tough times and inspired me to do more and want more out of life. Besides having the support system in my family, I valued having others around me who were willing to share how to move forward. They were not all great, however. Some gave me bad advice. Some became jealous and misused their power.

So, what do I think about mentors?

We all need mentors. We need others who have already been down the roads we are working to go down. We need more than just one because each person is going to have their own bias and opinions. You need a good assortment of people to ask questions and learn from. There are lots of great people that have done remarkable things in the world. We can learn about famous people's journeys. Or, get closer to home. You will meet different people every day who have done cool and interesting things. There will be lots of opportunities to ask them questions and learn about their accomplishments. They could include your family, parents, grandparents, aunts and uncles, or it could be coworkers or just someone you meet in an elevator.

As you get to know people and take time to hear their stories, you'll find so much to learn from their experiences. You need mentors with different perspectives and different life expectations.

Why do I say different life expectations? If what you want to do is bigger than what the person you're talking to thinks is possible, their advice might not help you get there. All these differences will give you some good perspective as you are working through life decisions. There are hundreds of different ways to get the same result. Everyone is good at different things. So, not everyone is going to do things the way that you do.

When I decided to draft this book, I did not know how to write or publish a book. I only knew one person who was a published author.

Randy Green has authored several books, the first of which is Colorblind. I asked him lots of questions and have appreciated his mentorship through this process.

BUILD A SUPPORT SYSTEM 171

I set out to learn from others. I started telling people I was going to write a book and they would say, "Oh, I know someone who wrote a book."

"Do you think they would be willing to meet with me and share with me how they did it?" I'd ask. Most people helped set it up.

I met with close to 15 people who had written and published books in a short time. One of them was this amazing woman who writes romance novels and let me tell you they are steamy. It is called the Angel Series by Jeni; the first book is Kellan's Sweet Angel.

She told me all about how she published her three books. She invited me to come to her writers' group, Village Lake writers. That was an amazing resource and I still learn from those ladies every month.

All these great people around me are doing wonderful things and I did not know until I started asking. Their opinions helped me decide how I wanted to forge my way through the book publishing world. A great way to find others to learn from is to ask yourself who you admire.

Whom Do You Know That You Admire and Why?

Think about that for a minute. Whom do you admire? It does not need to be someone famous.

I admire a woman named Catharine Gates who authored a book called The Confidence Cornerstone and started a nonprofit to support women to understand that they are important to God and that women's work is important to God.

It is so beautiful that she is sharing and helping the world in such a courageous way. I asked her to have coffee with me and we really hit it off. I have asked for some more of her time so I can learn more about how she published her book and help her mission in some way. She is a wonderful mentor.

All these different people had different paths they went down in their writing and publishing journey. They had varied reasons for writing. They had different beliefs. It really helped me decide how I wanted to go about it. If I had only talked with one person, it would have been hard for me to choose my path. I had to take all their advice and lessons and then decide what was important to me and what the right fit for me was. That whole story is for another book and still in the making.

Mentors for Different Areas of Your Life

My Great Aunt Catie, who I think was the smartest person in my family, always seemed to have the answers. She and her husband had gone to college and built a house. The rest of our family lived extremely poor. My Aunt and Uncle that raised me most of the time had six kids and took care of my grandpa in a 900-square feet house that my grandma left them.

My Aunt Catie was whom I called when I was growing into an adult, and I wanted life advice. She was the one I talked to about being a mom, my career, and what I wanted to do with my life. She was the one that I talked to about college and how much money I wanted to make.

I remember sitting in her living room when she asked me, "How much money do you want to make?"

I said, "I don't know. I want to make a lot of money."

"How much do you think is a lot?"

"$30,000 a year."

She went on to explain to me that she and my uncle each made about $40,000 a year at their jobs and that I should at least shoot for $80,000. She was the only one in my life who ever had such an honest conversation with me like that. She has been a great mentor. For a long time in my young life, $80,000 was my magic number. As I grew with my company, I went on to make much more, but I never would have gotten that far without that information.

There were also things I would have done differently. She refused to spend a penny on anything, she would not buy clothes or a new car. She still had a car with no AC. When she died, the first thing my uncle did was buy a new car and talk about how much she would have loved it. We get lots of good and bad from our mentors.

She passed away when I was in my late 30s. I felt very lost without her mentorship.

You will find the right fit for you. Foster those relationships. Take them to lunch or coffee and work to add value to their life as well. Be appreciative of their support. Make sure they know the value they are bringing to your life.

Coaches Are More Than Professionals

When you want to hit a big goal, especially if that goal is tied to financials, it makes sense to bring on a coach. Someone you pay to help you climb in the field they are in. You see, athletes always have coaches. Many businesses have business coaches. Executives have executive coaches. If you are paying them, you get serious about doing what they tell you to reach your goals. That kind of focus pays big.

If you are motivated like I am, you might just need an accountability partner. Becca, my best friend, is super smart and talented. When you want to get something done, she could be an amazing accountability partner. Becca is like the perfect blend of personal and professional. She is always happy, and solution-driven. She is dependable and always 5 minutes early. She always makes you feel inspired and like you can take on the world. She asks all the questions that keep you on track; focused and walking away with a clear list of 'to do's. When I have something that I feel is bigger than I can take on myself, she is my go-to person. She does not take any excuses and if you don't do it, well, that is on you. She loves you anyway.

Learn About Another Journey

I have met with several high-level executives as well as company CEOs just by asking if they would mind meeting with me to teach about their path. They share with you their journey and you can make decisions for yourself based on their path. I have found that almost any person at any level will meet with you to talk about themselves. They get to talk about them, and you learn valuable things to use in your life. It's a win-win.

Never Follow Anyone 100%

My daughter was about 12 years old. She was a good girl but very impressionable. She was going to a youth group at the school, and she was mesmerized by the leaders, Ram and Cindy. She thought they were so amazing, and she wanted to worship with them more. She wanted to worship on Friday nights and on the weekends. Well, I was one of those moms who was in her business all the time. Mostly because, where I grew up most girls were pregnant by fifteen and I wanted my daughter to get more out of life than that. When I dropped her off at their Friday night worship, my husband and I went in to check it out.

Turns out it was not a church at all. It was a section of an old storage building. It had a stage area and a big open floor. We let her stay but decided to go back and get her about 45 minutes early so we could interact a little.

When we got there to pick her up, we started asking for her because we did not see her. They seemed a little freaked out that we were there, like how a kid gets when they know they are going to be in trouble. As we were waiting for her, we were

BUILD A SUPPORT SYSTEM   179

looking around. There were all these teen girls laying on the ground with their eyes closed, worshiping or something. The lights were low so you could hardly see. There were back-room areas of some sort and every now and then someone would come out of another area. We did not see any adults. After a few minutes, my daughter came out of one of those backrooms and she was surprised to see us. She asked to stay for 30 more minutes, and I told her no. She did not even argue, she just got her stuff and even seemed to be in a hurry to go. When I tried to ask her questions, she just said they were worshiping. I am still to this day not sure what was going on there, but my daughter was busy every Friday night until she was eighteen.

These people had been approved by the school and were running an after-school church youth group. My daughter would have followed them to the end of the earth.

No one else's opinions or advice is more important than your own voice in your life.

At the end of the day, it is your life, and you have to live it the best way. Also, when you get it wrong you are the one who suffers the consequences. Take all the information and choose the best path for you.

You Will Outgrow Your Mentors and That Is Okay

Just as important as it is to have a mentor, it's important to know when to let go of a mentor. Sometimes in life we outgrow our mentors. We get to a place where we need a new coach who specializes in something different. As we grow, we change our minds and our path. It doesn't make those people any less important to you. You can keep them as friends. It's okay to decide that someone is not the right person to be your mentor anymore. If that is the case, start looking for new mentors. You're probably not going to have the same mentor throughout your lifetime.

BUILD A SUPPORT SYSTEM

I remember the first person that ever helped me understand what having a mentor meant. I was in my early twenties, and I had been working for this company for about 6 months. She was the first manager I had that believed in me. I had been accepted to transfer to a new store they were opening on the other side of the city. For the first few weeks, I was on the strap down crew. It means I was on knee pads on the concrete, pouring dish soap into the holes that the guys drilled with the drill gun so they could pound earthquake straps into the ground to hold the aisles up. It was a horrible job.

After 2 weeks of being on that crew she had the Cosmetics Department manager move me and told her I was too smart to be on the strap down crew. I didn't care much either way. I was surprised she thought I was smart. I had never even met her, and to be honest she was a little scary.

She had several conversations with me in the next month. She thought I was smart. She felt like I could do more. She helped me dream about my future. She had a bigger vision and could see potential in me that I myself could not.

She guided me as I grew into a Dept manager running the top-performing garden center in the entire nation. We had letters and banners and visits from every company that made garden supplies to say we topped in selling their merchandise. As a mentor, she gave me strength and inspiration, and took the time to have hard conversations to help me continue to grow.

One time she came to me and told me she was giving me a raise and I needed to put it into my 401k. I didn't even know what that was. At the time I was a young, single mom and did not even have the money for gas or diapers. I took her advice and 20 years later I cannot tell you how thankful I am for that mentorship.

There are a lot of amazing things about her and I never would have been so successful had she not come into my life. Early in

BUILD A SUPPORT SYSTEM

my career, I started as an hourly associate, followed by supervisor, then promoted to an assistant store manager. She had been a great mentor through all these phases. As I grew from an assistant manager to a co-manager and to a store manager, she was not the right mentor for me. As her life had changed course and mine as well, we grew apart. It always made me sad, but I knew that's just how life had to be.

Mentors are still people and have strengths and weaknesses. You pick up things you want to follow and things you don't as well. For example, my mentor did not believe in vacations or taking time off for family. She was a dedicated hard worker who would work herself to the bone and never ask for anything. That made her angry and resentful. I learned from her that my vacations and family time were important. Also, time off is what makes you whole, level-headed, and have a good sense of judgment to see the bigger picture. You cannot do that if you don't have any distractions, time to think, or do things to help you decompress.

We all need a support system. We need people around us to keep us going. They could change over time.

Pivotal Steps to Building a Support System

Step 1: Seek out mentors who are knowledgeable in your areas of interest.

Step 2: Decide if you need a coach or accountability partner to get yourself going in the direction you are looking for.

Step 3: Identify who your cheerleaders are and appreciate them for their support.

Chapter Thirteen

Who Do You Want to Be?

In this chapter, you will focus on who you want to be. What is it that you want? What would make your life better, easier, and more enjoyable? What kind of person do you really want to be?

To get the things you really want and move your life forward you will need to put away the negative self-talk, let go of what is taking up space in your brain, have a healthy relationship with failure and fear, believe in

WHO DO YOU WANT TO BE? 187

yourself, and be willing to ask for what you want.

Being your best self will not happen overnight. It will be a step-by-step process. It will be small things every day that get you there.

Project yourself into the future. Close your eyes and take a deep breath. Breathe in and out slowly. Then picture in your head what your best self looks like. The first time I did this, it just irritated me. I could see myself screaming "I don't know!" My best self? No clue.

But, Yes, you do. Breathe. Open your mind. You can do anything. Think about who your best self looks like and then add a little. Get out of your comfort zone and visualize a little more to the point where you are embarrassing yourself with your dreams. Just dream for a minute. Project yourself into your future self, three years from now.

If you could do anything in this world, what would it be?

- Do you want to be a teacher or a doctor or a firefighter?

- Do you want to serve your country in the military?

- Do you want to author a book or start a clothing line?

- Do you want to get a better job and make more money?

You already know about me wanting to be a retail store manager. What does success look like to you today? It may change over time. When I was young, success was graduating high school. Then as I grew, I wanted to be a store manager. Today, I want to be the author of a motivational personal development book that truly adds value to people's lives. It will change over time.

- Where would you live?

- Who would you live with?

- What kind of relationships would

WHO DO YOU WANT TO BE? 189

you have in your life?

- Where would you work?
- What kind of house would you live in?
- What kind of car would you drive?

To be your best self, you need to be clear on what you really want. I hope that this book helps you get clarity on what you want and guides you to get there.

Think about what a day in the life of your best self would look like. Start your thoughts with "I am, I do, I live, I drive."

What does my day in the life of my best self look like?

I live in a swanky, resort-style apartment in the middle of town with my husband. I drive a new, blue full-size Ford Bronco. I am the founder and CEO of a successful multi-million-dollar business, which I own and control. I get to interact with the readers of my New York Times best-selling book to hear their stories, and I can be a cheerleader for their accomplishments. I start my day with a perfect cup of coffee and spend a couple of hours on my next book, with my little pug cuddled up next to me. Then, I get ready for the business conference I am speaking at after lunch. I have great, supportive friends whom I go to lunch with regularly. Later in the afternoon, I spend time at the gun range with my son, practicing for our next shooting event over the weekend.

Take some time to dream about what your day in the life of your best self would look like.

We have gone over what your life might look like on the outside, now let's talk about who you want to be on the inside.

What does your best self look like on the inside? Are you kind? Do you show compassion to others? Here are things to think about as you are deciding who you want to be.

What Goes Around Comes Around. So, Treat Others How You Want to Be Treated.

You cannot control others, you can only control yourself. If you put bad things out into the universe, they will come back to you. If you act like a jackass to someone, you will spill your coffee on yourself, or your car will get backed into. When you put out negativity, you will get back negativity. It goes both ways. When you smile at someone, it causes them to smile back at you. When you are putting out positive vibes, positive things come back to you. Someone might buy you coffee, hold the door for you, or let you into heavy traffic. The more kindness and possibilities you put into the world, the more you will receive. What goes around comes around. Knowing that this is real, it is easy to understand why you would treat others as you would want to be treated.

Kindness Will Help Your Heart

When I was a store manager, I was promoted in October and Christmas was right around the corner. I am a pretty positive person, but that year my associates in my store were so crabby and not nice to each other. The next year I had more things under control and our store adopted some families for Christmas. We also joined with other stores and did fun things for our community. We dressed like elves and toured a special needs school, and my associates were so happy and filled with goodwill and holiday spirit. I could not believe the difference. We never went through another Christmas without reaching out and giving back to our community.

If It Doesn't Feel Right, It Probably Isn't

As you are working to be your best self, here are certain things to keep in mind. If it does not feel right, it probably isn't. Trust your gut and your instincts. Pay attention to your surroundings. People around you have all kinds of opportunities for you to support them, do things with them and learn from them. Also, pay attention to the people you don't want to be like and learn from them as well.

Keep in mind, you are working to be your best self for you. It matters what you are doing, especially when no one is watching. You are going to have to leave past mistakes or failures in the past and challenge yourself. You are going to grow and try new things. You are going to try things that are not going to work. I thought it would be cool to do belly dancing. Not so much. After months I was not any better than when I started.

Let's get into what your best self must look like on the inside.

- What are your strengths?
- What are your weaknesses?
- What gives you mental satisfaction?
- How do you talk to the ones you love?
- Do you reach out to others?
- Are you encouraging?
- Do you go out of your way to support other people?
- Are you consumed with your own goals and ignore what is going on in the world?
- How do you show love in the world?
- Do you spend your day talking about others in a negative way?

Remember you cannot change the past so let's not try. Manifest your thought in your future. Dream about what kind of person you want to be.

Here is an example of my best self. I work on being my best self every day. I have found that I need to make time to do things that fill my spirit. When you are doing things that make you feel good about yourself it has an influence on how you approach the world. I share here what that looks like for me and maybe that will inspire what it could like for you. Just remember we are all different. Yours could be completely different from mine.

Being my best self is to learn and grow all the time. Do things with all my heart. Be a meaningful member of my community (hence, I joined my local Rotary Club to do my part for my community). I work to build long and prosperous relationships. My best self looks like someone who supports others and helps uplift people around me. Especially women.

You see, I come from 17+ years of corporate America and we have done all kinds of nasty stuff to each other as strong women. Supporting each other was not something that was taught or practiced. I used to be one of those women who tore down other women.

I used excuses like, "I just don't get along with women."

But I now want my best self to be a genuinely nice person, strong and proud. I have learned to shoot a firearm, decided to write a book, schedule time for exercise, and constantly work toward moving closer to my best self which I am proud of.

Now I will ask you again, this time to write it down. What does your best self look like to you? What is that picture? Is there something you want to do differently in your life to be your best self?

You might only be able to think of one thing. You might not be able to see the entire picture. If that is the case, start with the one thing you can think of. Do something that makes you feel like you are being your best self. Watch for the green monster. As we discussed, it can lead you to what you really want. It takes time and practice not to react to others out of jealousy. One of the best ways to do that is to be your best self. Start with one badass day. There is a terrific book I highly recommend, You're a Badass by Jen Sincero.

Do something today that makes you feel proud. Do something that makes you happy. That could be anything. Planting a flower. Cleaning your room. Making your bed. Cleaning your desk. Doing something with your kids. Doing something with your dad. Do something that matters and is meaningful and makes you proud of who you are.

We have discussed in this book all kinds of things that hold us back. Ask yourself, "What is holding me back from being my best self?"

Work hard to zero in on what those pieces are that are holding you back. Diminish them so you can focus on what you really want out of your life. This might be the time you go back to a chapter that had things you want to work on, review it, and maybe even read another book that addresses that specific part.

Pivotal Steps to Be Your Best Self

Step 1: Imagine and write down who you want to be. Think about what you want in this world and who you want to be on the inside.

Step 2: Pick one thing to start. ACT on it. Do it!

Step 3: Do something kind.

Epilogue

WHAT COMES NEXT?

- Move: Pivotal Solutions for Your Life is published in English, Spanish and Japanese

- Keep an eye out for Windy Elstermeier's upcoming releases

    - Save: Pivotal Solutions for Your Finances and

    - Plan: Pivotal Solutions for Your Future

Afterword

My Ask From You

Please **share** what you found valuable in this book! I would love to hear from you!

- Send me an email at windy@pivotalsolutions.co

- Gift a book to, a friend, family member, colleagues or a mentee.

- Purchase this book for your team or a group.

- Write a review on the platform you purchased it on.

- Find me on Instagram @pivotalsolutions4u

- Find me on Facebook at PoivtalSolutionsAR https://www.facebook.com/PivotalSolutionsAR/

- Help me get this book to Oprah.

- Help me get it on the New York times best sellers list.

- Give me the opportunity to come speak with your groups. Email me at windy@pivotalsolutions.co

Acknowledgments

To all of you who helped and supported me through writing and publishing my first book. It was a huge lift and I could not have done it without every one of you!

My friends in the Networking community who inspired me to write this book. Melody Taylor, founder of Go Near Ministry (go-near.org) who was the last straw that made me actually get started. My dear friend Roger Elsheimer who read, edited, and cheered me on. My author friend Jeni, who I met after I started writing and has been a great support system thought the writing process including being an early reader and editor. My colleague, Rachel Korpella, Owner of Korpella Design (https://korpelladesign.com/), who designed my book cover and ideated with me to plan out four more books. My coach and friend Becca who project managed me to the finish line and was also an early reader and pushed me to reach out to Oprah and shoot for the New York Times best seller. Randy Green and Catherine Gates who mentored me through the year. My friend Angela Horton who was my cheerleader all the way and gave me the encouragement to secure my first book promotions events. Martha Londagin, who fiercely supported and encouraged me. My good friend Libby who listened to me talk about my book every week for a year and still loved me enough to run my social media campaign. My friend Jeremy who has known me since I was 12 and has always been a positive support and influence. Christal Dixon, who had weekly writing meetings with me. Nidhi Owner of Nids Creations who took the most amazing pictures of me. My Rotary Club who supported me and cheered me on every step of the way. The Village Lake

ACKNOWLEDGMENTS 205

Writers group who taught me many things about writing and self-publishing. Upwork at upwork.com who provided a platform to support all my needs through my writing journey with my final editor Sathammai Somasundaram and Jessica McNellis who edited the book and language translation services from Paula Dip who did my Spanish translation. University of Arkansas Global Campus Professional and Workforce Development who let me use their podcast room to record my audiobooks. Atticus, an author's best friend, without which I might have never finished. My daughter Brittany who called and showed me lots of love and support along the journey. Most of all my husband Scot, my son Noah, and my dog Pixel who laid next to me during every writing session.

About Author

They say 40 is the new 20 and I am living my best life!

I had an incredible career with a Fortune 500 company that raised me from an hourly associate into an amazing businesswoman. I went on to develop a variety of formats and emerging markets in over 800 locations across the U.S. I have had the opportunity to help grow amazing talent and support others while they grew bigger than they ever dreamed.

I have a strong moral compass and strive for long, prosperous relationships. I love what I do whether it is meeting new people, pioneering a company project, traveling with my family, or drinking my morning coffee. Oh, and I'm most proud that I have taught both of my children how to save money and be great cooks (My son makes incredible lasagna).

My company, Pivotal Solutions LLC, works to inspire and motivate others to be powerful in their own space. As a business coach, I work with people where they are, figure out what they need, and show up prepared to add value to their lives.

I am also writing a book to help inspire and motivate others to get out of their own way and achieve their dreams.

I am so grateful to have a wonderful family.

My husband and I have two adult daughters and a college-bound son. We have two rescue pugs, Pixel and Whiskey. We enjoy traveling to any place that has lots going on. We are big theme park junkies. Universal Studios is one of our favorites as we continue to go back year after year. We also enjoy culture, like the Museum of Science and Industry in Chicago and the Pike Place market in Seattle. We are looking forward to traveling internationally in the future. My husband of 20 years is a big foodie, and he wants to try all the best local food everywhere we go. We enjoy supporting our local community as we are Rotarians. Fall is our favorite time of year with such beautiful colors and great weather.